Contents

Foreword

It is with great pleasure that I write this foreword. Good management skills in a day nursery are so important as they enable a nursery to function efficiently. It is wonderful to find a book that contains information and training specifically designed for use in a nursery. Many people setting up nurseries will have little or no business experience and they will find this book essential reading. Practising managers and nursery owners will also find it invaluable as a skills check list and as a training guide for senior staff.

The book leads us through all the main skill areas touching on the legal requirements of employment and registration right through to organising a curriculum, parental involvement and marketing the nursery.

It is clear and concise and makes easy reading and I am sure it will encourage readers to look carefully at their own management practice.

Rosemary Murphy
Chairman
National Private Day Nurseries Association

Managing your nursery
A practical guide for nursery professionals

Ruth Andreski and Sarah Nicholls

A

publication

362·71

144146

Managing your nursery is designed to enable all early years workers to apply modern management principles in early years setting. It has been written by former Advisory teacher for preschool and nursery at Berkshire LEA, now a consultant and inspector of daycare nurseries, Ruth Andreski, and her colleague Sarah Nicholls, Lecturer and Early Years co-ordinator at Reading University.

Managing your nursery is the second in a series of practical books on management in early years settings. The first, Setting standards – a guide to achieving quality in the nursery, is available from Nursery World.

Acknowledgments

We would like to thank the following people for their help and support in writing this book. All those nursery managers who have provided material for the case studies but especially Melanie Godliman from Shinfield Park Day Nursery, Reading and Julie Kempster from Pangbourne Day Nursery. Bob Tychlik, who read our material on Health and Safety and provided additions and further guidance. Pauline Hansford who typed up the manuscript (from handwriting which sometimes left a lot to be desired!). Last but not least, our own families.

Published by Nursery World Limited © 1996.
Design, Tim Noonan; sub editors, Jane Lott and Judith Calver; Production, Gary Smith.
Managing your nursery **is available from Nursery World Limited, Lector Court,**
151-153 Farringdon Road, London EC1 3AD (sales hotline – 0171 837 8515).
Reproduced by Studio One Origination; Printed by Redwood Books.

Introduction

Whether you are an aspiring, new or established nursery manager, this book has been written to guide you through the maze of responsibilities facing you.

The valuable experience that you have already gained as a team member is fully recognised. Leadership, however, requires new skills and understanding. Although these can be acquired on the job through a mixture of common sense and trial and error, the application of established management principles, specially adapted to suit your needs, will enable you to function more efficiently and with greater enjoyment.

With nursery provision set to expand through the introduction of the nursery voucher scheme, it is essential that you are ready to face likely competition and validation procedures with confidence. In this climate, you need to know that what you are providing achieves the highest standards.

Each chapter has been written after consultation with practising managers who identified the particular areas of greatest importance for them. Authentic case studies should help you to identify with your own situation.

It is possible to use the book as a reference manual, concentrating on a theme that is most relevant to you at any one time. However, all the issues covered will prove essential reading for the manager who seeks to excel.

Ruth Andreski
Sarah Nicholls

CHAPTER ONE:

What is management?

Management is partly learned 'on the job', through your own experiences and from observing other managers. However, if you read this book and have a good, hard think about what is involved in nursery management, by taking advantage of the accumulated wisdom of practitioners, you will be able to avoid many pitfalls. By applying the underlying principles of management to your own situation you'll be more confident in your role. Above all, you should be able to focus on what matters and not be sidetracked by the hundreds of 'little things' that crop up daily in the life of a nursery.

Good management is about being efficient and effective. Effective means getting the right things done. Efficient means getting them done without wasting effort.

Four key skills are involved. These are:
● Planning
● Organising
● Leading and enthusing
● Maintaining authority

In the first two areas, there are several basic ways of behaving. They are:
Autocratic (I decide, you do.)
Consultative (I ask, you answer, I listen, I decide.)
Democratic (I or you ask, we discuss, we decide.)
Laid-back (I let my staff run the show – they're perfectly well-qualified.)

Some management theorists add a fifth way: **Situational** (Let's see what this situation demands and then decide).
    Generally speaking, in nurseries where staff are trained, knowledgeable and experienced, the best method of management is democratic. But not always. This is not to say that one minute you should be dictatorial; the next minute laid-back, so that your staff find you completely unpredictable. It is to say that planning, organising and decision-making do depend on the particular set of circumstances. Most often, you will find that being consultative or democratic produces the best results: it uses staff expertise and so is efficient and it keeps staff morale high. There are

times, though, when you will need to take the responsibility of making the final decision alone – that is your job – and times when you will want to stand back and let staff manage something on their own.

These various approaches stem partly from common sense and partly from management theory. One leading theorist of the 1960s, Douglas MacGregor, divided managers into those who believe that the average worker dislikes work and must be pushed into it and watched the whole time (Type X) and those who believe that people enjoy work, want to do well and only need support and encouragement (Type Y). The wise manager recognises that most people are somewhere between these two poles and adjusts behaviour accordingly. Another theorist, Abraham Maslow, demonstrated that while people work in the first place for money, there is quite soon a cut-off point after which they are not working solely for money but for job satisfaction. He was working in the 1940s but his work is still considered sound. Again, the wise nursery manager will find that allowing staff to exercise and extend their skills will give them job satisfaction.

PLANNING

A nursery manager will need to plan on several different timescales: the year ahead, the term ahead, the week ahead and the day ahead.

Weigh up the following management approaches to one simple planning decision. The matter under discussion is how can we encourage the four-year-olds to take more interest in books and give them an appetite for learning to read?

Approach A: The following written instruction is issued from the office to staff members of the Busy Bees (four-year-olds) Room:

> The Busy Bees will have a circle time immediately after rest time every afternoon. They should be organised into groups of five or six. During that time, the Kinderboxes of picture books should be made available to each group so that children can choose a book on an individual, pair or small group basis.
>
> They will be required to look at the books quietly for about 10 or 15 minutes and then be asked to comment on what they have liked about the particular book they chose.

A nursery manager will need to plan on several different timescales: year, term, week and day ahead

Approach B: A memo is issued to all staff members of the Busy Bees Room:

> I have been in discussion with the reception class teachers at the local infant schools regarding getting children ready for reading. They all have a time when everybody looks at books quietly for a period of

about ten minutes. I think that we could do the same here. I would, however, like to talk to you more about this at the next staff meeting, so please have a think about it before Monday.

Approach C: Manager talks informally with individual members of staff in the Busy Bees Room:

I think that we should be encouraging children to make more use of books in the book corner to help us and them to achieve early years curriculum targets. Can you give this some thought and come along to the staff meeting on Monday with ideas that we can all thrash about before we decide what we are going to do?

Approach D: Manager speaks to the senior nursery nurse in the Busy Bees Room:

Can you let me know what you have all chosen to do about encouraging children to use the books more? Then I can put it down in the nursery brochure for parents.

A is clearly highly autocratic and likely to cause staff resentment as it gives no recognition to staff competence and offers no scope for their ideas. B is consultative: it sets out the need clearly and invites input from staff at a pre-arranged time with a reasonable amount of notice. However, it implies that the method has already been decided on by management and comes in the form of a memo, which some people find impersonal. C takes a face-to-face approach, which is generally preferred by staff. Such a direct democratic appeal makes staff feel personally involved and also gives the impression that the manager is both highly involved and is treating the staff as responsible individuals with something valuable to contribute. D is so laid-back as to sound couldn't-care-less. This approach could lead to differences of method within the Busy Bees Room, which would undermine the achievement of all-important consistency for the children. It would also cut no ice with any outsider assessing the educational provision of the nursery.

ORGANISING

Both tasks and people need to be organised. This obviously involves thinking ahead, estimating and itemising what needs to be done and allowing enough time and resources to do it, allowing some slack for the unexpected. You have to have a clear idea of what you are trying to achieve and be brave enough to organise other people – your staff – to do a lot of it under your direction.

A new manager is usually selected because she is good at what she does now and because it is believed she has the latent ability to lead. However, the management post means that she must now move out of her comfort zone and stop doing what she did before. Her technical skills are now to be used to check that others are performing satisfactorily and to show by example how to do it better if necessary. If she carries on exactly as before, she will fail as a manager.

So the manager must decide what work is to be done and by whom; how it will be shared among individuals and teams. The manager must also organise liaison with clients and agencies in the world outside. To support all this, the manager must organise the administrative heart of the nursery, its office. Here records of accounting, client details (including children's records), policy statements, contracts and other employment records, correspondence, inspection reports and requirements, records of meetings and so on will all be kept in easily retrievable form. A well-organised office is essential, not just for efficiency but also to ensure that the nursery is complying with the law.

Consider the organisational implications of the following case studies:

A.   Lisa is not aware of the daily conflict between departments in the nursery. Those who work with the toddlers and three-to-five-year-olds accuse those who work in the baby room of taking an easy option. They point out that they have to keep more detailed records, based on observations, and have to plan activities in detail according to specific curricular aims. The staff in the baby room say that very little is spent on resources and equipment for 'their' room as all the money goes on the older children. They accuse Lisa of being much less interested in the babies.

B.   Since she was appointed manager six months ago, Maggie has nearly killed herself to make the nursery 'simply the best'. She takes on troubles and responsibilities from all quarters. She's working a regular 16-hour day and is, at present, enjoying the compliments showered upon her from parents and staff.

C.   Gemma has been in post for nine weeks. She divides most of her time between helping staff in each of the three rooms. That way, she says, she really knows what's going on with both staff and children. Her control of paperwork is, she says blithely, 'not too good – but people are more important than paper'. She is frequently in crisis time, rummaging through her overflowing in-tray for a particular piece of paper which demands immediate attention.

A well-organised office is essential not just for efficiency but also to comply with the law

A is a typical case of organisational deficit. If Lisa had apportioned work and resources fairly in the first place, such discontent would not have arisen. If she were more sensitive to her staff, she would have recognised or discovered that there was a problem sooner. She should now explain to staff why money has been allocated as it has and obtain feedback on the results of the present allocation.

Case B is of a manager who has not yet learnt how essential it is to delegate. She is not organising the workload, simply carrying it. Staff are 'delegating' responsibilities to her. Maggie will eventually suffer burn-out.

As for Gemma, she is refusing to recognise that she is now a manager. If she continues to stick to her 'comfort zone' of working directly with the children, daily life in the nursery will become chaotic and its direction confused. She must limit her time with the children and put her administrative responsibilities first.

> Do not be frightened that you are not a 'born leader'. Leaders are not born, they develop

LEADING AND ENTHUSING

Do not be frightened by the idea that if you are not a 'born leader', you cannot be a manager. One, leaders are not born, they develop. Two, if you replace the idea of 'leading the team' with the idea of 'managing the work of the team', you will be nearer the truth of what you need to do: to plan, co-ordinate, evaluate and praise.

However, you do need to:
- Believe in what you are doing.
- Be enthusiastic about what you are doing.
- Set a good example by eg not being late, being tidy, having high standards of practice, putting the children first.
- Make quite sure people understand you. Do your best to communicate clearly and to improve your communication skills if necessary.
- Be a good listener. Ask the sort of question that demands more than a one-word answer – eg not, 'How many years have you worked here?' but, 'What do you like best about your job at the moment? What do you like least?' When you are getting to know them, don't interrupt until people have finished talking. If they clam up, try to draw them out by repeating things that they have said and asking them to tell you more.
- Like the people you work with. Be interested in them.
- Praise good work. Praise in public, criticise in private.

SUSTAINING THE ETHOS

Ethos is about the feel of the place and is in large measure dependent on the quality of the manager. By way of illustration the following comments by her staff illustrate how one nursery manager succeeded in getting it right:
- 'We all pull our weight.'

- 'We have a lot of laughs.'
- 'We're not afraid to admit if we've made mistakes.'
- 'Susan [the manager] is always there to offer advice and support if we need it.'
- 'We praise each others' achievements.'
- 'We all like to keep the place looking half decent.'
- 'The boss notices and comments on a job well done.'
- 'If anyone's in trouble or needs help the others rally round – you never know, it may be your turn next.'
- 'If somebody doesn't agree with something, or wants to have a moan, they let it be known. We don't believe in bottling things up.'
- 'We actually socialise outside working hours.'

MAINTAINING AUTHORITY

It is the manager's job to implement policy, ensure legal requirements are met and to take ultimate responsibility. Her authority might be challenged by staff or by parents. A manager might react to such a challenge submissively – effectively giving in and losing respect – or aggressively, which will probably make for a head-on confrontation. The better alternative, if it can be managed, is to react assertively.

Consider these case studies:

A.   Sharon has worked for the nursery in the baby room for two years, since leaving college with an NNEB qualification. Her work was good until Marilyn joined the staff. Now they talk over the babies' heads, about clothes, boys, discos, TV. When reminded by another, older member of staff about the importance of interacting with the babies, they let it be known that if they were split up, they would both leave. It is hard to recruit qualified staff in your area.

Analysis:
Sharon has been loyal, but has perhaps become stale and bored. Marilyn appears the bad influence – why was she employed? What impressed you about her at interview? How adequately were her references taken up? Can you go back to her previous employer now? How likely is their threat of joint resignation to materialise? You hold the card that you will be writing their references. If you give in to their threat of resignation you will be perceived as weak and you will be failing the babies.

Possible action:
To impress upon them that they are failing at their job and that you will not stand for it. It is your duty to insist that they give the children in the baby room high quality

professional care. Consider sending either or both of them (separately) on a specific course of in-service training in baby care. A course is often very motivating and Sharon in particular needs a change and perhaps a 'reward' for her two years of good service.

B.   You have a little boy with special needs in your threes-to-fives room. He is funded by social services and comes from a very deprived and disturbed background. It is part of nursery policy to cater for such children. Several mothers form a deputation: they come into your office saying that they don't like their children coming into contact with Aaron as he sets a very bad example to their own children through his poor language and general behaviour.

Analysis:
This is a very difficult situation. Bear in mind that parents are challenging the nursery's policy, not you personally.

Possible action:
Take the parents' anxieties seriously. Talk to them calmly about the nursery's duty as a microcosm of society to integrate people with learning difficulties; that they are likely to encounter such children at school later. Explain that it is part of nursery policy to discourage swearing and explain the precise methods used by the nursery to do so, to give them confidence that every effort is being made to help Aaron become a more amenable child. Explain that if their children are instructed by their parents to avoid Aaron and do so in a very overt fashion, it is likely to make Aaron defensive and cause him to act in a more disturbed fashion.

Nobody's perfect – there will be times when things go wrong and projects don't quite work out. In such cases the manager needs to be resilient, able to bounce back and carry on, seeing mistakes as learning opportunities.

Finally don't forget the old adage, 'All work and no play makes Jack a dull boy'. A manager who doesn't recharge her batteries and enjoy her hobbies and the support of family and friends is doing her nursery no favours.

CHAPTER TWO:

Managing staff

'Any nursery is only as good as the people who work in it' (nursery school governor). A balance of staff needs to be struck between 'fresh blood' (A) and 'stability' (B). Too much of A produces:
- Confusion.
- Insecurity in the children caused by staff changes.
- Parental concern.
- Difficulty for the manager in implementing development plans for the curriculum, partly because of having to use management time for constant re-training.
- Money and time spent on job advertising and interviewing.

Too much of B produces:
- Lack of new ideas as staff get into a comfortable rut.
- Aging staff instead of a balance of ages.
- Fear of new developments.
- Staff insecurity about their capacity to adapt to a new situation.

RECRUITMENT

You must try both to match the person appointed to the empty job and to ensure that they will fit into the existing team. They should ideally offer interests and skills not offered by other team members. A good team is characterised by a balance of:
- Personality types.
- Interests and skills.
- Levels of experience.
- Age.

First, write a job description which details what the post holder needs to be (qualifications, ideal skills) and what the job actually demands. The job description needs to make clear to any applicant the full range of responsibilities involved in the post, expectations of the nursery and the minimum qualifications required. Reading this will help only suitable candidates proceed with applications.

Sample job description for nursery assistant:
- Basic childcare qualifications or a willingness to train.

- To support nursery staff by providing stimulation to the children, assisting in the care of toys and equipment and the preparation of food and drink.
- To help to maintain the safety, security and physical and emotional welfare of the children in the nursery.
- To work positively within the team structure and be included in staff duty rotas. Required to attend monthly staff meetings.
- To assist with project planning and implementation and with observation and record keeping of the children.
- Responsible to supervisor and deputy manager.
- To hold a current appropriate first aid certificate. To undertake training eg NVQ Level 2.
- To conform to the nursery dress code with respect to jewellery and footwear.
- To respect confidentiality within the nursery.
- To take on other duties as and when necessary.

Nursery nurse:
- NNEB qualification or equivalent. To hold or be willing to obtain an appropriate first aid certificate.
- To plan, organise, supervise and carry out a suitable programme for three-to-five-year-old children.
- To maintain a safe and secure environment for children.
- To settle in new children, liaising with parents.
- To maintain children's records.
- To supervise children at mealtimes.
- To attend staff meetings, assist with fund raising and any other duties the manager deems necessary.
- To keep abreast of current issues and attend training as necessary. Liaise with other professional bodies.
- To supervise students.
- To put into practice nursery policies.
- To work within a team and maintain good communication.
- To adhere to the dress code of the nursery.
- To maintain the nursery environment, including cleaning and other such jobs as may be deemed necessary from time to time for the efficient running of the nursery.

Senior nursery nurse:
- NNEB or equivalent with minimum two years post-qualification experience.
- To plan activities organised to suit children's stage of development.
- To maintain and administer relevant records.
- To maintain equipment and stock.

- To be responsible for certain elements of the budget.
- To be responsible for some health and safety routines.
- To supervise staff and students.
- To liaise with parents. Maintain and encourage parents' relationships with nursery.
- To assist with preparation and supervision of children's meals.
- To undertake staff meetings outside normal working hours.
- To maintain an appropriate first aid certificate.

These are general guidelines, providing a starting point from where they can be adapted to specific situations.

Advertising

From the job description, you should be able to write an advertisement for the post. The advertisement needs to carry certain essential information:
- Job title.
- Qualifications and experience required.
- Salary.
- Location and size of establishment.
- A description of the job and special features of the work – multicultural, emphasis on special needs etc.
- How and where to apply, including closing date. Don't forget the name, address and telephone number of the person to contact.
- Equal opportunities or similar statement of establishment philosophy.

Remember, the more you say in your advertisement about the job and your establishment, the greater the likelihood is that only suitable applicants will apply. A well-written advertisement will save you wasting time in interviews that will never lead to an appointment. Some specialist magazines will help you to write attractive copy at no extra charge.

> It is better to use a standard application form as this will ensure you receive the information you require

You must decide where to place your advertisement and how often it should appear. Consider first where the most suitable applicants are likely to see it, and advertise there. If you are not sure, find out where other establishments advertise similar vacancies. Look for a lot of similar jobs, and advertise with them. In recruitment advertising, the more vacancies that are advertised in one place, the better, because job seekers seek out media which carry the best selection of opportunities.

Shortlisting

When applicants contact you, send them a copy of the job description, terms and conditions of the post and details of the nursery (probably your information sheet or brochure). The terms and conditions include salary or salary scale, exact hours and holiday allowance. An invitation to visit the nursery is a good idea as well.

It is better to create or use a standard application form than simply ask for a letter of application as this will ensure you receive all the information you require before shortlisting (including all the information which you will have to pass on to the police and social services in order for them to provide the clearance which is essential before an applicant starts work). It will also make it easier to compare applicants. Your local authority will have standard application forms; so will personnel and some legal stationery suppliers, though you may need to adapt them.

Any application form should have plenty of space to state qualifications, previous and present employment, and reason for applying for a new job. An applicant must give name, address, date of birth, confirm that they hold no conviction which would prevent them working with children and supply the name, address and telephone number of two referees.

Once applications have come in, set aside a time to go through them all. Weed them out by asking:

- Do they have the necessary qualifications?
- What is their previous experience?
- Has the applicant presented him or herself well on paper? (A careless application might indicate sloppy attitudes.)
- Does the applicant seem to have an approach or philosophy which would be in harmony with your nursery?

Shortlist three to five candidates and immediately take up their references. You will waste a lot of time if you leave this until after interview. Most referees will be prepared to supplement what they say (or do not say) in the reference through a telephone conversation. If in any doubt, check a reference in this way. In the case of appointing your deputy, try to visit the candidates in their present placement and observe them at work; certainly find out as much as you can about them for such an important post.

Interview

Invite the candidates for interview on a date agreed by you and the other interviewer(s). Don't have too many co-interviewers and frighten the candidate; always have at least one other beside yourself. You might make up a panel from yourself, a senior member of staff, a parent representative, a member of the management committee and/or a local authority representative. An uneven number will ensure that a majority decision can be made if necessary.

Ask childcare/education staff to bring either samples of their work with children (this could be a photographic record) or a written example of how they would plan activities for a week for the age group concerned. Such a tangible contribution will

Ask any childcare candidates how they would plan a week's activities for the age group concerned

give the candidate confidence, inform you of their abilities and form an excellent basis for questioning.

Space the time at which each candidate arrives for interview so that they aren't tripping over each other. It will be informative and is probably essential to observe them interacting with the children (ideally this would be on a separate occasion). Such interaction provides other members of staff with the opportunity to note and feed back to the interviewer how they conduct themselves with the children and their perception of the candidate as a potential colleague.

You should decide on the length of time each interview will take beforehand and ask broadly the same questions in order to give candidates equal opportunities. Arrange beforehand which member of the panel will ask which questions.

When a candidate comes in, sit him or her comfortably, introduce the panel and give them an easy first question about themselves. Other questions you might ask at interview are:

- What do you feel you can offer the nursery in terms of special interests or skills?
- How would you go about generating a partnership between nursery staff and parents?
- How would you explain to a sceptical parent the value of play for young children?
- How would you care for babies to make them feel emotionally secure?
- How would you help children gain an optimistic view of the world and to increase their self-confidence?
- Do you think that nursery staff need to work as a team?
- Would you want to plan work for children with other colleagues or on your own? Why?
- How would you cope with a child who kicks you?
- Do you think it is a good idea to take children out of the nursery? How would you go about doing it?
- How will you keep in touch with new thinking and developments in nursery work?
- List a few books you particularly enjoy reading with children. Why do you like these?
- Would you accept this job if it were offered to you?
- If you wish to check that candidates are able to work nursery hours, you must ask all candidates the same question to avoid unfairness.

Remember that the order in which candidates are seen can influence outcomes (if a mediocre candidate follows two poor ones, she will appear more striking than she is). Interviewers must avoid making up their minds before they have seen all the candidates and had time to discuss them. Each interviewer could score each candidate's answers on a scale of one to five to make final decisions more objective. Good talkers can shine at interview: make sure their practice is as good as their prattle. Do not be influenced by irrelevant factors such as dress or accent, provided that they will not prevent a candidate doing the job properly.

Verbally offer the job to the chosen candidate as soon as possible, subject to police (criminal record) and health checks and a probationary period, usually of between one and two months. Never appoint a candidate about whom you have reservations. Once your chosen candidate has accepted the job, let the others know, not that they have been 'unsuccessful', but that 'I am afraid we have appointed someone else to this post'. Theoretically, no member of staff should start work until police and local authority health checks are completed; in practice, as there is often such a long wait, staff are allowed to start work provided that they are never in sole supervision of children.

You may think this a long, costly and over-thorough approach. Look at it this way. The cost of making a good appointment, advertising, say, in one local newspaper and one national magazine, then photocopying and posting information to, say, 30 applicants, plus one day's interviewing, perhaps paying travel costs to candidates, might be around £1,000. Quite a bit of your time, in the short term, will be taken up with fielding phone calls and queries.

However, the cost of making the wrong appointment, both in cash and in human costs, will be greater. The wrong person may be difficult to work with and cause others to leave. They may perform so poorly that you will be forced to go through the unpleasant process of dismissal. If they challenge dismissal, it may involve you in legal fees. You will be stressed, children disrupted, parents agitated, the nursery's reputation may suffer – hidden costs. Or the wrong person may simply leave quickly, and you will have to re-advertise anyway. Your costs will double, triple, quadruple. It really is worth making the effort to get it right the first time.

Once the candidate has accepted the job, follow up the verbal offer with written confirmation and a contract of employment (see Appendix one). Under the terms of the Trade Union Reform and Employment Rights Act 1993, you must provide an employee, within two months of their taking up an appointment, with a written statement setting out the main particulars of their employment. It should also contain a note of the procedure which will be followed in disciplinary and grievance procedures (see below). Pre-printed statements for employers to fill out are available from personnel or legal suppliers: as the law is very specific, this is a safe option. Clearly written guidelines to current employment law are in a series of booklets issued by the Department of Employment which can be obtained, free, from local Jobcentres.

Notice to any changes in particulars must be given to the individual concerned, in writing, within one month of the changes having been made.

> Make your new member of staff feel welcome and part of the team even before she starts

Part-time workers are now covered by the same legislation, irrespective of their hours.

Starting work

Make your new member of staff feel welcome and part of the team even before she starts, by providing her with any information she needs to absorb before she begins her job, such as copies of policies and procedures. If she can come in informally before they start, to meet staff and children and get to know her way around, it will make their transition smoother.

> Jack, a member of the original team that set up the nursery, was to leave after two years. His successor, Jill, was offered the job after a preliminary visit to the nursery, a formal interview and a longer session at the nursery, meeting children and staff. (Two others on the shortlist were also asked in for longer sessions, but at different times.)
>
> After accepting the job, Jill was introduced formally to parents (in Jack's absence) at the termly evening parents' meeting, when Jack's departure was announced. Later, she came to the nursery Christmas party to help and to meet parents and children informally.
>
> Jack was said goodbye to publicly, given a farewell present, etc. The changeover was handled smoothly for all concerned.

When a new member of staff begins work, identify a particular member of staff to show the newcomer 'the ropes' and make sure that they have been introduced to all other staff, including any part-timers.

Retaining staff

Research carried out by the authors of a National Children's Bureau publication, *Day nurseries at a crossroads* (by Jenni Vernon and Celia Smith, 1994) demonstrated the worst side of working life for some day nursery staff: low pay, relatively poor working conditions, demanding and sometimes exhausting work and the fact that working with young children is often perceived as lacking status.

On the other hand, the work is never boring, offers plenty of scope for people to be self-directed and creative in relation to the curriculum, offers the visible rewards of helping young children to achieve their potential as well as the fun and pleasure of life with small children. Parents generally, unlike the public at large, do appreciate the professional status of those who work with their children.

Against this background, the nursery manager is crucially able to influence staff morale and motivation and so their levels of job satisfaction. Practices which will help retain good staff may include:

- Making the staff room and toilet more than just utilitarian. Give these spaces attractive decoration, flowers, scented soap, any affordable details which make them a pleasure to use and make the staff feel valued.
- Rewarding ability and experience as well as responsibility within the staff pay scale.
- Always praising good work
- Keeping a birthday chart so that staff birthdays as well as children's are celebrated. Be aware, without being intrusive, of their private lives.
- Devising ways of injecting variety into peoples' work.
- Ensuring 'liveliness' through organising events, visiting speakers, ceremonies, outings, a photographer, perhaps the local press for some special occasion.
- Enabling and encouraging professional development through the stimulation and feedback of appraisal, training courses and delegated responsibility. Allow some staff time for planning and record keeping. Allow staff the chance to use and demonstrate their particular expertise. Invite them to offer their opinions and ideas.
- Maintaining a small library of relevant and up-to-date books and periodicals for browsing and borrowing.
- Being available to be consulted confidentially about work or personal matters.
- Staying cheerful, sounding cheerful and not frowning on staff exuberance. Allow people to express their *joie de vivre*. Bring a sense of humour to work.

> Minutes of meetings should be kept and action points followed up and reported back on

STAFF MEETINGS

One important way of ensuring good staff management and inter-staff communications is the regular staff meeting. Full staff meetings need to take place about once a month. Team meetings, of the sub-section of staff who work together, should take place more often, according to perceived need. Issues from team meetings can be taken to full staff meetings.

For successful meetings:
- Staff should be invited to add items to the agenda which the manager will then prepare and distribute.
- Everybody should feel they can contribute. Sitting in a circle is better than formal rows.
- Meetings should begin and end on time.
- The chair should keep control of the meeting and avoid time wasting.
- Minutes should be kept and action points followed up and reported back on. If they are not, staff will lose their trust in the staff meeting (See Appendix two).
- Promote the social growth of the team by organising refreshments – the best way may be to go out for a meal afterwards.

A staff meeting is the place where several things can happen:
- The manager can give important information to the whole staff.
- People can be publicly praised for good work or innovation.
- Issues that will benefit from a thorough airing can be raised. At times, it will be useful to ask each person in the room in turn what they think about a particular matter to ensure that everyone is having a say.
- Brainstorming to solve a problem.
- Decisions about the way forward.

APPRAISAL

At the other end of the personnel scale is the private appraisal interview. As the sound of this can make both appraiser and appraisee extremely nervous, it is important for everyone to grasp that appraisal is not external assessment of performance. It is to help staff develop and improve their professional skills via a planned process of discussing problems and setting targets with a supportive other person. Once someone has experienced appraisal, they rarely want to do without it: it becomes a service for their own personal development.

The generally perceived point and benefits of appraisal are twofold:

Individual
- Offers each individual a chance to assess their own performance: to identify areas of strength and areas of weakness.
- Gives an opportunity to devise strategies for improving areas of weakness.
- Enables the setting of aims and goals for career development.
- Gives individuals the chance to clarify how their job fits in with the overall team task, to establish priorities, air grievances or problems.

Group
- Enhances understanding of how the team fits together and how tasks are shared.
- Provides opportunities to adapt team organisation and/or aims according to changed need.
- Builds team morale and confidence; improves team communications.

However, it is not easy to set up an appraisal system from scratch with no experience. Some training is advisable; there are also videos and books devoted to the subject. If an appraisal system does not already exist you must first sell it to the staff. One way might be to hold a meeting to explain it, perhaps bringing in an outside speaker from a nursery which does practise assessment. On a board, have two columns, one headed 'Benefits', the other headed 'Concerns'. Invite all staff to suggest what any group of nursery workers (not just themselves) might put under those two headings.

Try to pin down which they consider most significant for further discussion.

Along with the general discussion of appraisal, stress that there is no one 'correct' system: the system that will work best is one that staff themselves devise and 'own'. Of course, this can be based on ones that have generally worked elsewhere (see Appendix three). The appraisal is usually carried out using the structure of a form based on a review of the appraisal period (which should never be more than a year) which the appraisee fills out a week or two before appraisal.

Such forms can be:

- Commercially produced from personnel stationers. This saves time, but might be more suited to business – though one could be adapted to suit your nursery.

- Devised by you and staff together. More initial work, but has the advantage that staff will feel that they 'own' the procedure.

- As above, plus using the job description to measure performance against. Or just use job description. This is both fair and tailor-made.

- Use or modify the headings for discussion in Appendix three. These are very detailed and consist of excellent practice. They represent very high aims indeed.

The appraiser then has a chance to consider the filled-out form and to prepare a short agenda for the appraisal itself. This agenda might include:

- Brief discussion of main points made.
- Further discussion on:
  a) item chosen by appraiser
  b) item chosen by appraisee
  c) item mutually agreed.
- Discussion and agreement on goals and aims – to what extent have current ones been achieved? Which should be those for the next year/term/other period chosen? An aim is a broad area of career development while goals are more specific aims within a particular timescale, usually identified as helping towards the broader aim.

  (NB Confusingly, other terms are sometimes used: aims called goals, goals called targets – make sure everybody in your nursery uses and understands the same terminology).

Up to an hour of uninterrupted time should be set aside for the appraisal. It should never be an interview; no-one should sit at a desk. Easy chairs at an angle to each other and cups of tea or coffee are the ideal. It is very important to use part of the time to focus on the strengths and improvements of the appraisee and to give unstintingly of praise.

This is a confidence-building exercise: if it is destructive it will be damaging and is better not done at all.

> Up to one clear hour should be set aside for the appraisal. It should never be an interview

Case study

Aims and goals set for Miranda Tempest, nursery nurse at The Isle Nursery, as a result of an appraisal session with Prue Spero, nursery manager. Transcript of summing up at the end of the interview.

Prue: So, Miranda. Let's recap on what's been said. I've noted things down as we've gone along, beginning with your strong points. You're a really good people person and therefore fit in well with the team. You are liked and respected by parents. Relationships with children are first class with good quality interventions. Finally, your contribution to the nursery environment has been positive.

If we turn to the future, your desire to become a senior nursery nurse is realistic and shows that you have a career vision.

Concerning the three things that we agreed you need to work on in the future:
1) Making a more effective contribution to curriculum planning.
2) Keeping more detailed observations for record keeping.
3) A need for more professional reading.

We are prepared to sponsor you on an advanced ADCE course, beginning with a curriculum module. Secondly, I will ask Amy to show you how she tackles the whole question of record keeping. And finally, we have a good staff reference collection in the staff room. Please use this to support your understanding of both curriculum and record keeping whenever you wish.

Shall we both sign what's been agreed?

Miranda: (signing) This is so different from what I expected. I'd been feeling really nervous that I was just going to be criticised.

Prue: Oh no. It's meant to be a celebration of your achievements and a plan of how to carry on the good work.

Managers will not want to avoid formal appraisal of their own performance measured against their job description. They need a chance to seek advice instead of always having the responsibility of giving it and they should demonstrate that they practice what they preach.

Where no system of managerial appraisal exists, ask your deputy, chair of the management or governing committee or other appropriate person to carry out the exercise.

GRIEVANCE AND DISCIPLINARY PROCEDURE

Even in the best-run nurseries, serious problems can arise. A grievance is a problem that a member of staff wishes to bring formally to your attention. The disciplinary procedure is a system laid down for dealing with a member of staff whose behaviour is threatening the satisfactory running of the nursery. The details of both procedures should have been given to new staff as part of their job statements. Use *Discipline at work*, the Arbitration and Conciliation Advisory Service (ACAS) handbook as a guide. The two most common causes of conflict among staff are:

- Personal animosity derived from such human failings as envy, jealousy and prejudice.
- Where one person has something to gain by putting down another. Check evidence for this!

If you find yourself dealing with such conflicts, use the following procedure:

Investigation
- Your line management structure should be clear. Nobody should have more than one boss. Do they?
- Listen to what people are saying by talking to them individually.
- Investigate the situation for yourself, drawing on the opinion of others if necessary.

Resolution
- Open discussion or arbitration. May involve moving personnel.
- Use policy documents to support decisions. In particular, use the provisions of the Children Act with reference to putting the needs of children first.
- Reasons for your conclusions need to be made clear to parties involved.
- If the conflict stems from outside the nursery, individuals must be reminded that it cannot be allowed to interfere with their professional lives.

Case study: Julie's grievance
Belinda is nearing retirement and has been at the nursery for 25 years. Recently, she has had a lot of time off for 'a bad back' which lasts for two to three days at a time. When she returns, she says, 'I mustn't bend, otherwise my back will go again'.

Other staff, particularly Julie, who is in the same room and junior to Belinda, are complaining that she is not pulling her weight.

Possible course of action:
- Listen to Julie's complaint.
- Verify the situation yourself by observation.
- Discover whether Belinda has sought or is currently receiving appropriate medical treatment.

- Insist that Belinda seeks appropriate treatment.
- While Belinda is receiving treatment, Julie must be supported with extra help or compensated for extra workload.
- Analyse working procedures to see if Belinda can temporarily carry out a more sedentary role.
- Remind Julie that we all may have problems at one time or another but reassure her that you are keeping the situation under review.
- If no improvement occurs within your pre-set time limit or if it is clear that Belinda's condition is not susceptible to medical intervention and can only deteriorate, discussions must be held with her as to whether she is able to continue with her present post. Is there an alternative within the nursery that extra training would enable her to fulfil? If not, you will need to look into the legal and financial processes of early retirement.

Case study: Verbally warning Sharon

Sharon, the newest member of staff, has missed three of the last five staff meetings. Excuses range from other, unexpected, engagements to, 'I have a migraine'.

Possible course of action:

- Remind Sharon of her obligation under her job description in her statement of employment to attend meetings.
- Enquire fully into her reasons for missing them.
- Remind her that these professional duties must take precedence over private engagements.
- Remind her of her duty to her colleagues: meetings generate their own tasks and she cannot be allowed to opt out.
- Monitor subsequent attendance.

In these and in real cases, a record needs to be kept of the action taken.

CHAPTER THREE:

Financial management

However good other aspects of nursery management, if the financial side breaks down, the nursery does too. Some nursery managers may have part of their financial management burden handled by another agency, but it is essential to be aware of the whole picture. Fees or grants will come in at one end and be disbursed in a myriad of ways. Money in and money out has to be recorded and accounted for in detail, whether to satisfy auditors or the Inland Revenue.

To discharge all your duties of care and education satisfactorily, you will have to formulate a purchasing policy that reflects your priorities – parents won't be impressed by a new carpet in the staff room if the climbing frame is falling to pieces, to give a crude example.

Development plan
This will highlight priorities in spending over the coming year and should avoid ad hoc and inefficient use of money by targeting it towards purchasing of equipment, staff training or alterations to the environment.

Book-keeping
Good book-keeping minimises an accountant's time, and therefore charges, and enables you to remain in control of finances. An accountant or business adviser will probably be the best person to advise you on the right book-keeping system to suit your particular circumstances. Ready-made systems can be bought from good stationers; alternatively, but more expensively, there are some excellent software packages designed specifically for the nursery manager (look out for advertisements for suitable packages in *Nursery World*).

Before investing in any computerised system, get representatives from different firms to demonstrate their wares to enable you to match capabilities against your needs, both present and, if you can anticipate them, future. The outlay for a computerised system may seem high, but, particularly in a large nursery, it will save you a lot of administration time, particularly if you are planning to do the payroll yourself: this can eat up time. A personal computer and good software package will do more than just accounts. You can use it for documents of all sorts, including standard letters, and for many purposes, from a database of names and addresses which will automatically print labels, to supervised use by children.

Whatever book-keeping system you use, you will need:

- A record of income from whatever source – grants, fees, allocations, subsidies, fund raising, etc.
- A purchase book in which all purchases and their date are recorded. You may need to differentiate between capital costs and running costs for tax and your own purposes.
- A record of expenditure with all entries backed up by invoices and receipts on file, each one with a record of the cheque number that paid it or a signature confirming a cash payment.
- A bank statement file.
- A wages and salaries record including National Insurance records.
- An Inland Revenue file for all tax returns and records (if applicable).

BUDGET CONTROL AND MONTHLY BUDGET STATEMENT

The conventional system is to call each area of expenditure a 'Head' and to allocate each Head a sum of money at the start of the financial year. To plan a budget forecast, estimate the amount of money you should have coming in. Unless it is completely certain that you will be full to capacity with a substantial waiting list, estimate conservatively, assuming you will have between one and five places empty, depending on the size of the nursery.

Predict expenditure based on the previous year's, but with a percentage increase corresponding to likely increases in your costs to take account of pay rises, increases in utilities charges and insurance premiums and so on. Plan those areas where you know you will be spending more money than the previous year – for new equipment or other capital expenditure, for example, and, if necessary, compensate by allowing less in another area. Be realistic. Allow a sum for contingencies (unexpected expenses).

Keep a monthly budget control sheet on the lines of our example overleaf and at a glance you will be able to keep a check that expenditure is going according to plan.

With this information collated on one form you can see at a glance whether expenditure allocation is going according to plan and it will enable you to satisfy yourself that your forecast is on course.

FEE COLLECTION

It is essential that you receive your fees promptly, otherwise you will, at best, be losing out on the interest that fees in an interest-bearing account will earn and, at worst, be running up an expensive overdraft in order to pay staff salaries and other bills on time.

BUDGET CONTROL SHEET				
Receipts	Budget	Actual	Budget	Actual
Fees				
Grant				
Milk subsidy				
Fund raising				
Dinner money				
Interest				
Total receipts				
Employers National Insurance				
Food and supplies				
Light and heat				
Telephone and alarm				
Equipment Play				
Kitchen				
Functional				
Nappies				
Building Maintenance Cleaning L L = labour M = materials M Total				
Windows L M Total				
Garden L M Total				
Bank charges				
Advertising				
Training				
Printing and stationery				
Postage				
Miscellaneous (detail)				
Insurance				
Publications				
Subscriptions				
Contingency fund				

A budget based on the previous year's expenditure is an essential tool in financial management. A monthly budget control sheet, such as the one shown on the left, will then tell you at a glance that everything is going to plan

The most efficient way to ensure fees are paid on time is to:
- Require them to be paid by a certain date, such as no later than one week after the start of term.
- Levy a financial penalty for late settlement.
- State that children will not be allowed to return to nursery if fees remain unpaid.

Don't hesitate to have a rigorous procedure for chasing up late fees. The following stages are a guideline:
- Penalty for late payment, as above.
- A polite reminder letter.
- A stronger reminder letter.
- A threat of action in a small claims court.
- Actual litigation in a small claims court.

You cannot afford to allow your clients to think they do not need to pay you, however hard their circumstances may seem. Once word gets around that 'they don't really do anything', others may be tempted to default. What you can do for true cases of hardship is let it be known that you will accept staggered payment – perhaps weekly or monthly instead of termly.

Wherever possible, ask parents to pay by direct debit, which saves a great deal of administration time. You could encourage parents to agree to this by pointing out that it will help to keep costs down and/or by giving those who pay by direct debit a very slight fee reduction or some other incentive.

If your payment system is based on the actual time a child spends with you and you invoice afterwards, make sure, as above, that you state a date by which payment must be made and impose a penalty for late payment.

REGISTRATION AND NOTICE

Some nurseries prefer not to charge registration fees, believing that they may deter parents; others see it as a way of ensuring that parents do not frivolously put a child's name down (and perhaps of earning some useful income). You will know best whether a registration fee is useful in your area. You could have a registration fee which, if a child takes a place at nursery, is counted towards their first (or last) term's fees but is otherwise not refundable.

It is essential to fix a period of notice that parents must give before withdrawing a child, otherwise your financial planning may be undermined. Normally, parents

You cannot afford to allow clients to think they don't need to pay, however hard up they seem should let you know at, or before, the beginning of a term or month that their child will leave at the end of that term or month. If not, it is normal to require fees in lieu of notice, or not to return any deposit that parents paid at the outset, though you may in practice be flexible about this if you have confirmed that you can fill the unexpectedly empty place.

INSURANCE

Re-assessing your insurance may mean you end up by spending more on your premiums, but this is probably better than being under-insured. Make sure that as well as the insurances that you legally must have (employers' liability and public liability) you are happy with the type and cover of others. You might want to hold: equipment, business interruption (or loss of income), personal, key person, credit, buildings, frozen food, loss of money and personal accident. Every two years at least you should check your inventory of equipment to re-assess the replacement cost. If your insurance cover has been with the same firm for some time, ask for quotes from other companies and make sure that any no claims bonuses are being taken into account. Three organisations to contact for help are the British Insurance Brokers' Association, the Personal Investment Authority (formerly FIMBRA) and the Association of British Insurers (see Useful Addresses at back of book). Many childcare organisations arrange specialist insurance at advantageous premiums: do look into these.

If your insurance has been with the same firm for some time, ask for quotes from other companies

KEEPING A TIGHT REIN ON SPENDING

You can waste a lot of money without realising, either by not adding up the 'little bits' or by failing to find more frugal ways of managing. Ask yourself the following questions:

- Can stock be suitably stored? If access to the cupboards is poor, items can be forgotten. If they are too small, materials such as paper and card can be spoiled.
- Are staff sufficiently careful with multi-item pieces of equipment, making sure that they are put away in complete sets? (It is, of course, part of even the youngest child's education to follow this practice.) In many cases, if one part is missing the whole activity is spoiled and needs replacing.
- Are you wasting energy? The ways of doing this are too numerous to list. You can obtain free advice from the Department of the Environment's Energy Efficiency Office on 01345 247347, from a variety of local initiatives (check with your local authority) which may include one of the Local Energy Advice Centres administered on behalf of the Energy Saving Trust by the National Energy Foundation, or from gas and electricity companies.
- Are your bank charges too high? This is a notorious complaint for small businesses. Shop around all the banks, building societies and Post Office to discover which would be the best account for you, with the lowest charges. At the very

least, you should be able to obtain free banking for one year before charges are levied. Keep as much money as possible in an interest-bearing account but do not allow your current account to be overdrawn – the costs are ferocious. It is possible to set up a system that automatically transfers money from your deposit or other interest-bearing account to your current account when the current account drops to a certain level.

● Are staff making too many personal phone calls? It is better to install a payphone for them than find yourself with a vast phone bill that you have to argue about afterwards.

● Do you regularly monitor your building for a 'stitch-in-time' repair policy?

PURCHASING POLICY

● Never buy goods or services for the first time without getting at least two alternative quotes first. You are not necessarily looking merely for the cheapest, which often proves false economy; you are looking for the best value.

● Discover if you will get a better deal for some item or service which you need regularly if you become a regular customer. This will involve negotiating: you offer your regular custom in exchange for a discount.

● Do you need to buy this thing? Do not be seduced into expensive equipment for every activity – sorting materials, for instance, can be carefully collected rather than expensively bought. Some dressing-up clothes can be found at jumble sales as well as in specialist catalogues, but make sure you wash them thoroughly. Creativity and problem solving are better achieved by providing children with tools and materials with which to make things for themselves.

● Can you get a better deal by banding together with other purchasers?

● Do you use the cash-and-carry?

● If you prepare food on the premises, remember to buy in-season fresh fruit and vegetables. Especially when there are chest freezers or deep cupboards, a surprising amount can be wasted by failing to use old stocks before ordering new. Observe 'use by date' criteria on stock, perhaps with the aid of a stock control book.

● Be aware of what parents do. A range of expertise and enterprise exists among them which you can tap for the nursery's advantage.

● Look further than conventional educational suppliers for some items, eg silver sand from builders' merchants.

● Have your questions worked out when you contact suppliers so that you give the impression of someone who knows what they want.

Discover if you will get a better deal for some item or service if you become a regular customer

FUND RAISING

Fund raising is more appropriate for some nurseries than others – it would probably be out of place in a workplace or other nursery where parents pay high fees, except for some special project. However, in many community nurseries or those which form part of or are a registered charity, monies gained from fund raising form an essential component of the budget. Quite apart from the fact that fund raising makes equipment and interesting trips available to those who otherwise could not afford them, it encourages valuable social interaction among those who organise events. They may be:

- A parents' committee or 'Friends of XYZ Nursery'.
- A staff/parent committee.
- Staff alone.

The parents' committee provides a focus for parental co-operation but will probably need some staff liaison. The staff/parent group gives important messages to parents about mutual commitment.

The following are all tried and tested money raisers:

- Summer fêtes and barbecues for all the family.
- A summer outing by coach to a place of interest.
- A garden party with teas, stalls and sideshows.
- A nursery picnic and fun day.
- A harvest festival, Diwali or Eid supper.
- A Guy Fawkes party (obviously high security needed for this one).
- Parents' dances or cheese and wine parties.
- Dress, jewellery, make-up, etc sales.
- Nearly new and jumble sales.
- Auction of promises (where one member of the parent body offers a service, eg to mow a lawn, bake a cake, make a frock, baby-sit, and this is auctioned to the highest bidder).
- Sponsored events in nursery time eg trike ride round the nursery garden.
- Bazaars or 'fairs' of various kinds – particularly useful around Christmas.
- Christmas parties.
- Theatre trips organised by the nursery, which can take advantage of discounted group bookings but charge parents the full ticket price.
- The nursery can act as a children's clothes/books/toys exchange, taking commission on items sold. Or as an agency, drawing a small fee, for an inter-parent baby-sitting group.

You will need to take out a public liability insurance for such activities, but this is not expensive.

If you think that such fund raising could contribute significantly to your budget, you will need a good committee, with a chairperson, secretary and treasurer. Either ask for volunteers or have an election. Even if parents or 'friends of the nursery' actually do most of the hard work, they will appreciate staff support, and particularly that of the manager.

It is important to publicise for what the committee is fund raising. Parents are better motivated if they can see the aim will directly benefit their children. The manager's job is to identify items that the nursery needs for which parents can fund raise, to be gracious about the whole business and to ensure that parents are publicly thanked afterwards, perhaps through a newsletter, a parents' meeting or by displaying the item in the entrance hall with a notice.

GRANT SEEKING

This might be the job of the nursery manager or of a deputed committee. The manager will need to be involved as items like audited accounts, a statement of aims and a statement of needs are almost always required to be submitted.

As above, grants and donations are not necessarily appropriate to every nursery. They are available from various sources, including:

- Local authorities (usually from the social services and education departments).
- Charities, trusts and other grant-making bodies with a remit to help children. Find details of ones appropriate to you at your public library in eg *The voluntary agencies directory* (Bedford Square Press).
- Local businesses which are sometimes happy to make goodwill gestures to the community, particularly if a little local publicity can be arranged.

The advantage of grants is that quite reasonable sums of money can be raised at a stroke without huge efforts to get the parent body galvanised. Sometimes grants are 'matching', that is, awarded after the nursery itself has demonstrated its commitment by raising a matching sum.

Grants are generally made with specific conditions attached to their spending (that they are used for specific needs, that mention of the grant-making body is made in nursery stationery or publicity) and the nursery will need to report back, demonstrating that the money was spent in the way expected.

Approach your local business and industry community to divert their useful waste to you

FREEBIES

Offcuts of card, waste paper, remnants of material, old furniture and storage, even old computers – these are a few of the items that find their way into the dustbins of factories, offices and small businesses. Find out if you have a Scrap store in your area which sells just such items at a very reasonable price. Or approach your local community of business and industry, by letter or, probably more effectively, in person in order to divert such waste to you. Managers of enterprises are usually moved by the idea of helping small children. Be prepared to collect materials immediately the donor says that they are ready as part of the deal is that they want a clear space. Don't forget to say thank you afterwards.

Case studies

These are examples of four different nurseries with some different budgetary and managerial requirements. You should be able to find one example near enough to your own situation for you to be able to gain some ideas to help you. The phrases in bold represent key issues which have been discussed above.

A.   Steeple Road is a community-based nursery. It caters for parents who mostly wish their children to attend on a part-time basis. Some are working mothers, others use the nursery because of family circumstances or to enable their children to experience what the nursery has to offer. The nursery receives an annual grant from the local authority, which subsidises needy parents.

Kim, the manager, has a complicated financial management task. She is answerable to a management committee with its own treasurer. She presents a **monthly budget statement**, which includes the current situation and that of the equivalent month the year before. In order to do this, her **book-keeping** procedures have to be impeccable and easily-read. She finds it well-worthwhile to employ a professional book-keeper who, for a relatively low fee – which works out at £12 per hour – translates all the information recorded in her books into computer-printed statements.

B.   Is a small, independent Montessori nursery school. It takes in 24 children aged two to five years. It is totally reliant on the fees it collects from parents. Melissa, the owner/financial manager has a clear policy on **fee collection**. The survival of the nursery depends upon her getting her financial planning right. She bases her budget on four fewer children than she is registered to admit, to give her some leeway. She relies on the paid services of a chartered accountant and believes he saves her far more than he costs in fees.

Melissa keeps a **tight rein on expenditure** while ensuring that the nursery is properly equipped and maintained. She has also worked out a careful **purchasing policy** in order to minimise costs.

C.   This nursery is attached to a college used by a considerable number of mature students, some of whom have children under five who form the nursery clientèle, attending while their parents go to lectures and seminars. Although the college subsidises the nursery with an annual grant, this is not sufficient to cover its running costs and fees are collected from students as well. With so many part-time children, Rosalind, the manager, has a complicated task in collecting fees, keeping her staffing levels right and working out wages and salaries. Although she has the advantage of 'losing' some of the service costs of the nursery, as the college picks up the heating, lighting and water charges, her budget is limited and she relies heavily on **fund raising** and **freebies**. She has also worked out a careful **purchasing policy** and finds it useful in reducing costs. She is also careful to make sure that expenditure is balanced between the four departments (based on the age of the children) into which the nursery is organised.

D. This is a nursery attached to a school. It caters for children aged three-to-five-years. The head teacher and governing body allocate a sum of money to the nursery for equipment and materials (building and other running costs come under the school's budget). Alison, the nursery teacher, and Fiona, the nursery nurse, have to take a long view of their requirements since the funds come at the beginning of the school year and there must be no question of them 'running out'. They also have to plan and claim their budget a long way ahead. Their two major considerations are **balancing expenditure to cover all areas of the nursery curriculum** and **targeting expenditure to fund their annual nursery development plan**.

CHAPTER FOUR:

Policy, procedure and practice in childcare and education

Policy: A course of action adopted or proposed by an organisation or individual. What you would do in particular circumstances.

Procedure: A mode of performing a task. A series of actions conducted in a certain order or manner. How you would do it if you had to.

Practice: The application of policy. Actually doing it in the way laid down in your policies and procedures.

Nurseries that have devised their own policies, procedures and practices are more likely to be efficient, to be able to ensure greater consistency for children and to avoid misunderstandings with parents than those that are making it up as they go along, with different individuals freshly attempting to solve each problem as it arises. Creating policies, procedures and practices takes thought and work, but will save staff time and stress later.

The creation of written policies should be a team effort, to ensure a sense of ownership and therefore commitment, but the team should be led by the nursery manager or officer in charge. This person needs to put policy decisions into a written document and make sure that everyone either has a copy or knows where the documentation is kept or displayed. Students and volunteers should be asked to familiarise themselves with the nursery's policies and some or all of them should be made available to parents (probably by displaying them on a board or filing in a clear plastic envelope in a portfolio).

There is a statutory requirement to have three particular written policies. A legal minimum is very different from good practice. The list below includes both categories; those required by law are marked with an asterisk.

Good practice would dictate that nurseries have written policies on:
- Admissions
- Waiting lists
- Illness and exclusion
- Staff responsibility during emergencies
- Health and safety*
- Children's behaviour

- Reporting suspected child abuse
- Personnel policy (including appraisal and training issues)
- Volunteers – their role and responsibility
- Equal opportunities*
- Procedures for delivering and collecting children
- Children's records*
- Code of practice for special education needs.

Validating inspectors for the nursery voucher scheme will be interested in your written policies and their implementation.

Procedures are also needed for:
- Marking attendance
- Reporting accidents
- Recording menus
- Keeping staff files/information
- Producing written contracts with families
- Drawing up an annual development plan
- Managing finances.

POLICY MAKING

There are a number of key principles to bear in mind when producing your policies:

Relevant legislation
The manager needs to know existing legislation and be aware of any debate around it, in the shape of impending amendments, draft documents and consultation exercises. She needs to do this because:
- Parents and colleagues will come to her for advice.
- She will need time to prepare the nursery for change.
- It is a way of participating in policy making – no good moaning after the event if you did not respond when consulted.
- Failure to comply with the law may lead to eventual closure.

In order to achieve knowledge and understanding, the manager needs to read informative newspapers (both local and national), her professional press and attend meetings and seminars organised by professional groups.

> A manager needs to know about existing legislation and be aware of any debate around it

Requirements of good practice
In any policy, bear in mind the paramount importance of health and safety. Be as certain as you can that you have thoroughly thought through issues in each policy.

Team involvement

If a policy is to work and be effectively practised by all staff, it is essential that the team is involved in its creation.

Workability

All policies must be realistic and clearly related to your own nursery, although referring to abstract principles. You may use someone else's policy as a starting point, but if you simply copy it, the necessary team involvement will not have taken place. A policy must be wedded to everyday practice.

Foresight

No policies are set in stone. They need to be reviewed and modified in the light of experience

This is the imaginative capacity to envisage exactly how it will work in practice. You need to consider a wide variety of situations which might occur and to ask yourself, 'What would happen if...?' and to write your draft policy in the light of the answers you arrive at.

Clarity

Every policy must be written in clear, uncomplicated language that everyone can understand. It must be unambiguous, succinct and well laid out on the page for ease of reference.

First draft

Early discussions will result in a first draft that can be put out for consultation, particularly with parents or their representatives, so that any modifications can be made in the light of their suggestions and practical experience. Once you are happy with the draft policy, you might wish to share it with others who might be affected by it and gain their views – local schools, other nurseries, daycare advisers, providers of services, etc.

Final draft

This can be duplicated and issued to all the staff and added to the policy portfolio or noticeboard (parents should know where either of these are). New parents need to know the nursery's policies so that they can make an informed choice.

Review

No policies are set in stone. They need to be reviewed and perhaps modified in the light of experience, new information or new legislation.

Case study 1: Criteria for teams to consider when developing a behaviour management policy

The need for such a policy is self-evident. It will promote consistency among staff; if shared with parents, it will hopefully also promote consistency by all the adults who are significant to the child. Psychologists and childcare professionals stress that consistency to young children is of vital importance for their satisfactory emotional development.

Possible issues of concern
- Aggression towards other children.
- Aggression towards adults.
- Non-compliance.
- Failure to co-operate with other children in the nursery (including an unwillingness to share).
- Spoiling materials and equipment.
- Spoiling activities.
- Verbal abuse/swearing.
- Withdrawn behaviour.
- Displaying unnatural sexual awareness/behaviour.
- Difficult behaviour at mealtimes either with the food itself or in the manner of eating it.
- Temper tantrums.

Strategies
When devising strategies that can be consistently applied by different members of staff, knowledge of child development is crucial. Children go through similar stages in socialising basic instincts, such as those of territory and ownership (exact age-related details of this are spelled out in *From birth to five years: Children's developmental progress* by Mary D Sheridan (NFER 1973 and Routledge1992) but much of their behaviour is learned.

Nursery professionals will need to consider:
- Role modelling by adults.
- Different parenting patterns.
- The importance of expressing feelings.
- Giving appropriate outlets for children's energy.
- The influence of experiences, eg literature, TV, computer games.
- Being realistic in our expectations.
- Communicating our expectations to children.
- Being firm and fair.
- Developing a child's positive self-image through praise and encouragement.
- Criticising a child's actions rather than the child.
- Encouraging nurturing behaviour and empathy.

Case study 2: Scenarios to promote group discussion of equal opportunities
Do you know where you would stand in law with regard to the following?

- Wanted: Young lady, committed to the care of children under five, to work in Nettlefields Nursery. Telephone Mrs Braithwaite, Nettlefields 123456.

- Telephone conversation: 'Look, we don't want a blinking homosexual working in this nursery. I tell you, if we take on this man, every single parent will take their child away and then there won't be any nursery for him to work in anyway.'

- 'At storytime, we feel it's nice for the children to sit with their own community group. Mary takes the Afro-Caribbeans, Susan the Asian children and I take the white ones from round here. It seems to work very well.'

- 'We get the girls to clear up, they are so much better at it. Then, while they are doing that, the boys are allowed to run around to let off steam. We do ask them to put away the bikes and large equipment when they've finished.'

- Dear Mrs Blake,

    I have to express my grave concern at what I saw in nursery yesterday when I came to pick up James. He was walking around in a pink dress and a woman's hat, with high-heeled shoes on his feet and a bag in his hand. I must ask you not to let him dress up in this way again. It could lead to severe psychological problems, he might even become a transvestite or homosexual.

    Please give me your assurances that such a situation will not arise again. I would like to see him doing male activities like football or woodwork, not being turned into a little girl.

    Yours sincerely,

    MC Anderson

- Required: an assistant for the above nursery, must be fluent Urdu speaker and fully conversant with the customs of the Pakistani community.

- Christine is confined to a wheelchair. Some members of the staff think she should be employed in the nursery, others don't. What do you think?

- Dear Mrs Ogilvey,

    Thank you for your recent letter requesting placements for some of your child-care students.

    We confirm that we would be delighted to offer two placements but, having

regard to the philosophy of our nursery, would request that you do not send anybody from the ethnic minorities.
Yours sincerely
A Person

- Ms Muffet has been a playgroup supervisor for many years. She recently qualified, through private study, and would like to set up her own nursery. Since she knows so many parents in the neighbourhood, which is racially mixed, she feels she does not need to advertise other than through word of mouth, among her friends and neighbours. In this way she believes it will be a truly community affair ie people with similar aspirations and way of life.

- Our cook is a really motherly sort of woman. She says, 'All the children here need a good, hot lunch and all this fussiness about funny meat and no pork is rubbish. Just cut it up fine and the children won't know any difference, let alone tell their parents.'

- 'I'm not having that child Winston in the nursery because his parents are trouble makers. They complained about us to the Race Relations Board.'

- Nursery regulations
  'All children are expected to wear our own little uniform. Exceptions cannot be made under any circumstances. Girls: regulation skirts and t-shirts, white ankle socks, black shoes. Boys: grey shorts, white shirts, white socks, black shoes. Girls and boys are expected to wear hats/caps respectively.'

- Dear Mr Patel,
  Thank you for your letter requesting a place for Mitesh at our nursery.
  Unfortunately, we feel that we have to refuse on this occasion as this is a very English nursery, with only English children attending it, and we do not think that Mitesh would be happy here. We suggest you contact one of the nurseries nearer your home where, no doubt, there will be a lot of other children from the Asian community.

- Dear Mrs Allison,
  I sent my child to your nursery because I wanted her to learn about English things. I am not happy that she has been eating Indian sweets and doing all sorts of strange things from another religion. We are Christians and are displeased that our child is practising what we regard as pagan ceremonies.
  Perhaps you would let me have your assurances.

CASE STUDY 3:
Notes on equal opportunities policies compiled by different practising nursery managers

Policy 1

- All activities are offered to both boys and girls.
- The Nursery operates an equal opportunities policy and pledges not to discriminate in terms of
  a) race
  b) gender
  c) disability
  d) culture
  e) religion
  f) sexual persuasion.
- Children should be aware that different races exist.
- Children are encouraged to partake in all activities, regardless of their gender.
- Children are encouraged to be tolerant of people with disabilities and not to discriminate against them.
- Children should be educated about cultures and religions other than their own.

Policy 2

- Each child is unique and treated as an individual regardless of gender, race, culture, religion and special needs.
- We will encourage children to learn about various cultures.
- Children, regardless of gender, will be encouraged to express themselves in all aspects of play and encouraged to learn to work together co-operatively and constructively.

Policy 3

In our nursery every child is to be treated as an individual. All religions and cultures are respected and reflected in the nursery. Equal opportunities are given to all children by means of artefacts, books, posters, etc. Nursery activities enable both the gifted child and the child with special needs to explore and learn about the multicultural and multiracial society in which we live.

Policy 4

Equality of opportunity will be given to every family with regard to their creed, colour or race.

This policy will be adhered to with regard to staffing and the care and education of each child.

We will comply with all polices that have been issued by social services and the Children Act 1989.

Policy 5

No child will be discriminated against in terms of religion, culture, disability and gender.
Religion: Children will learn about a variety of festivals as part of our nursery curriculum. We celebrate Christian festivals (state if you wish your child to be excluded).
Gender: We will offer multicultural activities/toys. No toy will be denied to any child. All children will be encouraged to play with any toy within the nursery and both genders will be encouraged to participate in tidying up.
Staff: Management will appoint suitable staff regardless of gender, religion, race, age, colour and disability. Management reserves the right to support suitably skilled staff after a probationary period.

Policy 6

Our nursery operates an equal opportunities policy. As we live in a multiracial, multicultural community, no child will be discriminated against because of their race, religion, gender or ability. All children will be treated as individuals.

CHAPTER FIVE:

Keeping records

Some records are legally essential (eg a register, so that you know which children are in your care at any time, staff tax and National Insurance details), some are required if you are to be taken seriously as a preschool educational establishment (eg children's developmental records) and some you simply couldn't function without (eg your waiting list).

Running the records is an essential management task. They can be kept manually in a filing cabinet, which can be locked for security and confidentiality, or on computer or a combination of the two. Some should be subject to more security than others and as soon as any records are computerised, they become subject to the provisions of the Data Protection Act. You need to be aware of these provisions: you can find out more from the Data Protection Registrar, Wycliffe House, Water Lane, Wilmslow, Cheshire SK9 5AF.

All records pertaining to a particular person should be able to be seen by that person if they or their parent/guardian wish, so they should be written in clear, professional language – no slang or slander.

These are the records that should be kept:

CHILDREN'S RECORDS

Waiting list: When a parent registers their child, you need to record certain essential information to enable you to make contact and to help make the decision about when the child might start/when they might attend. A waiting list registration form should include:

● Parents'/Guardian's name, address, telephone number (both work and home).
● Child's name and date of birth.
● Hours and days wanted for child.
● Any other comments.

You might want it to include:
● GP, health visitor or other professionals' details.
● Record of immunisations.
● Whether child attends any other childminder, playgroup or nursery.

The waiting list should be kept in chronological order of registration so that you can operate on a first-come, first-served basis, though you may need to temper this according to your child-age/number of staff ratio, whether you keep some places for priority cases or other criteria. This will depend on your admissions policy (see chapter four). It is also helpful to keep another list in alphabetical order so that you can easily locate the records of a particular child.

Registration form: Once a parent has accepted a place, you will need to gain full information (some details may have changed since the waiting list, some to give you a picture of the child and enable you to help the child to settle, some for medical reasons and some in case of emergency).

A registration form should include:
- Child's full names and date of birth.
- Parents' names and (if different from child's) addresses.
- Child's address.
- All telephone numbers applicable.
- Parents' place of employment and work contact telephone numbers for both mother and father.
- Names, addresses and telephone numbers of two responsible people appointed by parents in case you cannot contact parents in an emergency.
- Child's GP: name, address and telephone number.
- Child's health visitor.
- Immunisations.
- Any medical conditions; details of any medication that the child needs to take at nursery.
- Contact with other carers eg childminder, playgroup, nursery..
- Siblings and their location during the day
- Any special dietary requirements.
- Any information needed for child's well-being eg pet name.

Health record: For ease of reference you will probably want to keep these separately, perhaps in a card index near the phone. Likely details are parents' and GP's contact numbers, details of vaccinations, allergies, dietary restrictions, medication and any medical condition from which the child suffers.

> For ease of reference you will probably want to keep health records separate from others

Registers: It is best to buy formal registers so you can keep a clear attendance record, for health and safety reasons, in case of emergency evacuation, to ensure correct billing and to keep track of a child's general attendance.

Reports: When the child leaves you, it may be required and it is anyway good practice to write a report for the establishment the child is moving to, highlighting physical, social, emotional and intellectual development. These can be written up from the ongoing reports that will have been kept on the child and shared with parents at regular intervals.

Ongoing reports (formative records): These should have a series of observations noted and dated under the headings of physical, social, emotional and intellectual development which are summarised (summative records) at intervals to be shared with the parents. For schools this is usually termly (sometimes half-yearly); for nurseries where children are developing so fast, we suggest every four months.

STAFF RECORDS

Individual staff: You should keep a record containing the following:
- Name.
- Address and telephone number.
- Next of kin, address and telephone number.
- Previous employment.
- References and social services/police clearances.
- Salary.
- Entitlements.
- National Insurance number and Inland Revenue reference number and district (this information may be with payroll records).
- Holiday dates, absences and sick leave.
- Appraisal records (see chapter two).
- Other information.

For forward planning, you will need a chart of any staff holidays that take place outside nursery holidays and cover organised. You will need records for temporary staff as well as for permanent.

CURRICULUM/ACTIVITIES

Babies: The aims for each baby and the activities that will achieve these aims should be written up following their periodical devising by staff, so that they can be referred to and a record made when they have been achieved.

Toddlers: The same is true for toddlers, and it should be remembered that everything that occurs within a nursery should follow a developmental continuum so that the children gain from different and stepped activities.

Three plus: Here, the activities should reflect a full nursery curriculum developed under the following headings – personal and social development, language and literacy, mathematics, knowledge and understanding of the world, physical development, creative development (see chapter nine).

The records should cover the structure of the curriculum, materials, activities, topics covered and useful references as well as each child's own record of achievement.

EQUIPMENT

A list of all the equipment in the nursery will be needed for comprehensive insurance cover and stocktaking purposes (see chapter three). You will need to restock on a regular basis: divide equipment and supplies into that which needs restocking daily, weekly, monthly, quarterly or yearly, so lists can be ordered and checked off as appropriate.

Books might have a separate list, if you think it worth the bother. There are some classics – eg *The very hungry caterpillar* – which you may want to have multiple copies of in a larger nursery. If you borrow from a library, you will need a library list in order to make sure that no books go astray. If you send books home with older children for shared reading, you will need a record of what has been issued to whom.

For large/expensive pieces of equipment, you will need a record of details of purchase, guarantee, warranty, repair and replacement cost.

NURSERY

Records here will relate to the building and will obviously vary according to the degree to which you are responsible for it, varying from ownership to simply using it. Whichever, you are likely to be responsible for services such as telephone/fax, heating, lighting, window cleaning, cleaning services and will want relevant records, including monitoring of costs to check they do not deviate from target.

You will find it useful to gather information relating to other nurseries and agencies and essential to have records for social service and other local authority contacts, professional associations and training establishments with whom you have links.

You will want records relating to the nursery kitchen, of menus in case of any health enquiry, and to ensure that the diet is balanced and varied, and of food stock to avoid waste (see chapter three).

You will want records relating to the nursery kitchen, of menus and to ensure the diet is varied

FINANCE

Depending on who is doing the books, you may need records relating to:

● Accounts, including staff salaries and wages
● Invoicing
● Cash receipts (see chapter three for more detail)

Balance sheets and forecasting are essential management tools. If you plan to computerise, make sure you choose a software package that can manage all these things.

BOOKINGS

If you ever hire out your facilities, you will need to keep track of rental, insurance and payments that relate to the hire. Also, bookings for nursery excursions or special events will require records to be kept.

CORRESPONDENCE

Keep a copy, on computer or file of standard letters relating to admissions, head lice, etc in order to save time. Date stamp letters received and staple photocopies of the replies to important ones. File all correspondence to be on the safe side, but you will sink under paper if you don't have fairly frequent clear-outs of routine, out-of-date stuff. Don't forget to keep a postal record.

CHAPTER SIX:

Time management

'I felt like some kind of butterfly, flitting from one thing to the next, constantly interrupted and never being able to get on with the jobs I set out for myself on that particular day.'

Josephine, Manager of a 50-place nursery

It is a common complaint of those in managerial positions, wherever they work, that their day is spent sorting out first this, then that, all the time being interrupted and asked for comments, opinions and action. But is this detrimental to being a good manager?

One excellent way of analysing the situation is to make, as Josephine did, a time log of one or more working days. She did this in order to see if she could detect any patterns or bad habits and find any ways of changing things to give herself more control over her time and thereby become more efficient.

JOSEPHINE'S TIME LOG

TIME	ACTION
8 - 8.30 am	Unlocking doors, greeting staff, parents and the plumber,who has to be shown where the leak is in the older children's toilet. Informal chatting with several parents.
8.30 - 9 am	Answering telephone about a child who will not be attending today because he has earache. Begin to go through the mail but have to abandon it because a staff member asks if I could look at a child's rash. I look at the rash, I think it is German measles. Phone mother to to ask if she can take child to the doctor to confirm.
9 - 9.30 am	Return to office and start looking at the mail all over again! Answer telephone call from local authority inspector, who would like to visit next week. Note this in nursery diary to advise staff. Plumber informs me he has finished and asks me to sign his job sheet. I inspect the work with him, then sign.

9.30 - 10 am   Show new parents round the nursery with a view to registering their child. Spend some time talking to them in the office about our programmes and philosophy.

10 - 10.30 am   Continue talking to parents. They want to come, so go through enrolment procedure, collect registration fee. Work out wording of advertisement for a new member of staff to replace TF. Phone local paper with ad.

10.30 - 11 am   Finish with mail, throw some away and write three letters as necessary responses. Phone secretary of our local nurseries group re a professional evening later this month. Talk to cook, check on lunch (we have been worried about our cook's performance lately – some children have not enjoyed their food and parents have complained.

11 - 11.30 am   Phone potential speaker for our next local network joint in-service training evenings and confirm programme. Write letter confirming. Start to work on the invoices for parents. Parent of child with suspected German measles arrives, I talk to her and accompany her to her car as she takes her child away.

11.30 - 12 noon   See start of lunch, I am satisfied with the meal today. Take cheques from the filing cabinet. See deputy and advise him that I am going to the bank. On way, member of staff advises me that a child has fallen and banged his head. Will I look and administer first aid? I do, child OK now. I record accident in the book.

12 - 12.30 pm   Proceed to bank, pay in cheques and obtain petty cash for the week.

12.30 - 1 pm   Eat snack lunch at desk! Do a bit more on the parents' invoices. Look at staff orders for new equipment. Answer phone – it's the mother of the child with suspected German measles – a confirmed case.

1 - 1.30 pm   Prepare notice about German measles to put on nursery door and write letter to all parents to inform them. Photocopy enough for distribution.

1.30 - 2 pm Resume work on staff orders. Check the catalogue for best prices. Begin to write orders. Walk round nursery again, interact with staff and children.

2 - 2.30 pm Carry out appraisal interview with Melissa C.

2.30 - 3 pm Appraisal interview continues, we agree current situation and identify ways forward and training needs. Phone call from local college re student placements. Lecturer wonders if she can pop round now. I agree.

3 - 3.30 pm Write a few more orders for the staff. Lecturer arrives, I show her round and we discuss mutual expectations. We agree to have two placements.

3.30 - 4 pm Go and observe LS setting up a display for children. Discuss and advise, she agrees she will be ready for formal NVQ assessment in a couple of weeks' time. We agree date and I enter it in the diary. I put the German measles notice on the door.

4 - 4.30 pm Phone call from parent who will not be able to pick up her child on time, advises me that a Mrs Z will be coming instead. I advise right person. Amanda B comes to the office and asks me to stand in for a few minutes as Sarah is crying and needs to compose herself. Sarah has a boyfriend problem! I agree. It gives me a nice opportunity to play with the children in her group.

4.30 - 5 pm Rep arrives with his wares.

5 - 5.30 pm Secretary of management committee returns draft policy on 'bringing and taking children from the nursery' which the committee has accepted with one additional suggestion of its own for inclusion.

5.30 - 6 pm Out and about in the nursery to greet parents, be available for informal discussion etc.

6 - 6.30 pm See last children and parents from the premises, say goodbye to the staff, gather up those orders into briefcase to take home and finish – together with shift list for next week. Lock up.

This time log exercise proved extremely useful to Josephine. It revealed that her day was highly varied, divided into a considerable number of short-term (often ten-minute) activities. It showed that she is fully employed throughout the day doing the things which managers do ie planning, organising, encouraging staff and actually being 'in charge'. It showed that she is the person to whom others within the nursery come for advice and the person whom people from the outside world approach first, as the representative of the nursery.

Josephine need not worry too much about being 'some kind of butterfly'. It is characteristic of the manager's role, whether in nurseries or other enterprises, that they do move from one activity to another in fairly rapid succession.

However, Josephine's time management techniques are not perfect. The log reveals that her time is divided between that spent reacting to other people's demands and that which she controls. In other words, although many of the things which Josephine does are planned, others are not. She should try to increase controlled time and reduce reaction time so that trivial issues do not drive her off course. She cannot and should not try to abolish reaction time: reacting to events is part of the work of the manager. The skill is in identifying the correct way to react.

> She should not try to abolish reaction time: reacting to events is part of a manager's work

Josephine should not have gone home with work in her briefcase. It was a long day and she needed the evening free in order to be mentally fresh for the next day.

How could she have avoided wasted time or time mis-spent in order to keep the evening for herself and feel calmer during the day?

● Have staff trained in health and first aid matters so they could have dealt with German measles identification and the child with the banged head themselves.

● Have ready-prepared infectious disease letters for parents to avoid having to produce them at short and inconvenient notice (as a pro forma letter in the computer or as a master copy only needing the date changed for photocopying).

● Delegate equipment procedures – there was a monkey (see following section on delegation) if ever there was one. Staff would have looked at the catalogues for inspiration, price comparison, etc when recommending new equipment for purchase. Having approved the choices, Josephine should have got them to fill in the order forms and calculate costs at the same time, leaving her free just to check them.

● Josephine should not let commercial representatives turn up out of the blue. They should make appointments.

● Consider 'blocking' times for parents' visits – or a special time for new parents.

DELEGATION

Though vital, this is a surprisingly difficult thing for managers to do. It involves giving authority to others and yet being ultimately responsible for what they do. Managers may fail to delegate for a variety of reasons:

- New managers may be nervous or unskilled at issuing requests to staff.
- Managers may feel that no-one else is capable of doing things properly.
- Managers may fail to plan enough time to explain/train about what it is that they hope to delegate and to establish that colleagues and they are on the same wave-length, so end up doing it themselves.

Alternatively, they may delegate inadequately:

- By simply issuing orders so that colleagues
  a) feel small and
  b) don't necessarily understand the broader picture, therefore don't offer helpful suggestions or work in context.
- By not communicating effectively so that they may very well end up with the wrong results.
- By not providing feedback ('That was good, thank you; that wasn't quite what I had in mind, could you explain what happened?') after tasks are done so staff both feel unappreciated and do not learn from experience.
- By never delegating anything challenging so that other members of the team are not able to develop their skills and abilities and therefore do not become stronger members of the team. This is a vicious circle.
- By delegating to inexperienced members of staff without confirming that they have the capacity to carry out the task.
- By not spreading the delegation load fairly across the whole staff. It is unfair to overload one competent member because another avoids extra work (there is such a thing as learned helplessness). If a manager delegates too much, it can lead to charges of managerial laziness or even exploitation, which will do the nursery's reputation no good and cause good staff to avoid it.

The benefits of delegation are considerable. Managers who delegate:

- Have time to concentrate on the most important elements of their job – keeping the nursery on course to carry out its aims and fulfil its plans.
- Provide valuable experience for staff seeking job satisfaction and/or promotion. Cause their team to become stronger and therefore more supportive and better for the nursery.
- Enable the organisation to run smoothly even in the manager's absence. If the manager is ill, attending a course or otherwise absent, she won't spend her time worrying that the nursery is falling to pieces.

> Managers who delegate have time to concentrate on the most important elements of their job

Reversal of delegation

In popular parlance, this is called 'passing the buck', though in this situation it is being passed back to the manager. On management courses it is often referred to as 'passing monkeys'. Such monkeys – which must be fed and cared for – rightfully belong with the member of staff to whom they have been entrusted. If managers find they are being asked to look after someone else's monkey, they must politely return it immediately, albeit after offering advice on its care.

PRIORITISING

A manager should frequently ask – almost certainly at the start of each day:
- What are the most urgent things?
- What are the most important things?

Urgent things need to be done immediately but may not need much time devoted to them and may not need to be done by you. Important things need enough time and though they may not have an immediate deadline, must not be put off being started as they are of true significance. Leaving them to the last minute because you have been distracted by things that simply shrieked louder or interested you more is sloppy management.

Make a list of objectives at the end of the previous day or the beginning of a new one. Be analytical and rank items in order of priority. Fit in new ones that crop up according to their urgency/importance. As the day goes by, tick off completed items. Beware of confusing 'less important' with 'things I don't like doing much'.

Within this framework, establish a method for dealing with daily paperwork. Divide each crop of post into:
- Not of interest or use, throw away immediately.
- Of interest or use to another member of staff, pass on.
- **For action:**
  Immediately.
  To be replied to during letter-writing session.
- **Needed for reference:**
  Can be remembered – read and throw away.
  Can't be remembered – file.

Rank items in order of priority. Fit in new ones that crop up according to their urgency/importance

Policies and procedures

Having written and known policies and procedures (see chapter four) will save you a great deal of time. Other people will have to refer to you less frequently to check what they should be doing and you will be able to use the policies and procedures to guide you through much problem-solving.

Information technology

Time spent in learning to manage a computer will easily repay itself by later saving time on tedious administration. Most paperwork can be held and produced by computer faster and more clearly than you can produce it yourself and this saves you from having to produce it from scratch.

Three important questions to ask yourself:

● Am I spending too much time in meetings which are not profitable to the nursery? (The Institute of Management/DHL *Finding the time* research report of March 1995 gave as one of its ten conclusions that successful managers 'Hold action-centred meetings, not talking shops'.)

● Do I write letters when the same result could be achieved by telephone?

● Do I make a decision on every piece of paper that crosses my desk the first time I see it? There is evidence that the average manager delays action on 60 per cent of all the daily in-tray items which could have been disposed of at first handling (see RA Mackenzie, *The time trap*, McGraw Hill, 1975). Since The Industrial Society's 1993 survey *It's about time* discovered that 26-33 per cent of management time is spent on paperwork and that 90.3 per cent of directors/managers work with a cluttered desk, it is clear that taking immediate action would improve the situation enormously. But there is no point planning a quick whip through the post if, for example, your finance report for your management committee needs revising for an 11 am meeting. In such a situation, you must prioritise.

Sacred time

A manager should try and set aside ten minutes of not-to-be-disturbed time each day. Develop the habit of using them for reflecting, making judgements, having new ideas. No-one in charge should become so overwhelmed by events that these few moments of control are beyond them.

CHAPTER SEVEN:

Marketing your nursery

You may not like to see your nursery, based as it is upon caring for children in a gentle, non-competitive atmosphere, as a business. Sadly, we can assure you that if you do not promote your business (the nursery) and keep its product (excellent care and education for children) in the public eye, you will find a competitor (another nursery) stealing your success and your profits.

You are in the world of marketing. Marketing requires that you:
- Know your product.
- Know your customers.
- Know your competitors.

Then you will need to know how, where and when to advertise.

Analyse your product
You need to address the following questions:
- What is special about your nursery provision?
- What age of children do you cater for? Be specific – how many of each age group?
- What hours are you open? Again, be precise – are you offering all hours for all the children?
- How many weeks of the year are you open? When do your holidays fall?
- How is your nursery organised? Identify facilities – different rooms, office, outside. Consider its location and any significance this has in relation to transport.
- What is your staffing? List everyone and their qualifications, where they work and with which children.
- How much do you charge? Per session/day/week/month/term?
- What do the children gain from being at your nursery? Identify five, clear over-riding aims.
- Where do children tend to go on to from your nursery?

If you answer these questions honestly and in detail, you will have a very clear picture of your nursery.

Analyse your customers
Knowing exactly who they are will enable you to concentrate on building on this market (building on strength) and identify if clients you think should be represented are not. If not, you will have to devise a strategy to attract them.

The children:
● How many do you have?
● Of what ages? Does one age group predominate?
● Do they have younger siblings?

The parents/carers:
● How many married couples do you serve?
● How many co-habiting couples?
● How many single parents?
● How many adults are in full-time employment?
● In part-time employment?
● Unemployed?
● Is there a predominant employer, union or group?
● What areas do your children come from? How far do they travel?

This may all seem self-evident, but perhaps you may have some surprises when you calculate your predominant customers in actual numbers rather than relying on a rough idea.

Know your competitors
● Write down all the nurseries you know of in your immediate area.
● Research the existence of further ones by checking places such as Yellow pages, Thomson directory, libraries, social services, local authority education department, local advertisements, etc. Ensure that you cover the whole area from which your customers come.
● Get copies of their brochures.
● What do your competitors offer that you do not?

Decide what you do best and what you offer that others do not, adjusting if you think it wise

Decide what it is that you do best and what you offer that your competitors do not, adjusting your practice if you truly think it wise and you can sustain it. At this stage, you can write your brochure, if it needs revamping, and consider your advertising strategy.

Prepare your brochure
The following headings will help you:

- The **aims** of the nursery in terms of its care and education of children (this is required under the validation of the nursery voucher scheme).
- The **philosophy** of the nursery (what's so special about you?).
- The **curriculum** of the nursery:

  How young children learn, through their senses, observation, experiences, etc.

  Play as a means of delivering the early years curriculum.

  The areas of learning ie personal and social development, language and literacy, mathematics, knowledge and understanding of the world, physical development and creative development.

  Delivering prereading and prewriting skills.

  Linking in with the National Curriculum.
- The **organisation** of the nursery. This could include:

  How the children are grouped and an explanation of the key worker system.

  Staff and their details (though if you don't want staff turnover to make your brochure outdated, you could mention staff only in general terms eg number of staff, type of qualifications).

  Daily routines.

  Meals and mealtimes.

  Education through play and planned activities; type of equipment.
- **Partnership with parents.** This could include:

  The partnership agreement (see chapter ten).

  Admissions procedure and waiting list.

  Home visits if applicable.

  How we can help your child in nursery/how you can help at home.

  Regular dialogue, both formal and informal.

  Arrangements regarding delivery and collection of children.
- **Health and hygiene:**

  Diet and feeding.

  Weaning.

  Dress.

  Nappies.

  Toilet training.
- **When a child is ill:**

  At home.

  In nursery.

  Occasions when you would have to exclude a child.
- **Behaviour and discipline.**
- **Your links with the local community and other agencies.**
- **Meeting the needs of individual children.** This might include:

  Special needs, including gifted children.

Equal opportunities for boys and girls.

Equal opportunities (race/culture/religion).

- **Fees, including terms and conditions and systems of payment.**
- **Policies and procedures** (details of how copies can be obtained and read).

The design of your brochure will carry quite a few messages to parents. At its simplest, it might be a few typed and duplicated pages of information; at the other end of the spectrum, a glossy publication. Either might be appropriate to your market; parents will draw their own inference from how expensive-looking the brochure is. But, even simply typed pages should be well laid out and easy to read, not squashed together in a small type face, and could be interspersed with children's drawings. There should be no spelling mistakes. Never issue a brochure that has not been read by at least one other person in order to make sure it is completely clear and unambiguous. If you plan an ambitious brochure, it would be well worth your while to employ a graphic designer's assistance – though make sure you obtain quotes first.

Depending on the name of your nursery, you might find your own logo, or symbol, a great marketing aid. It could decorate your stationery, sweatshirts, mugs and be a clear identity for your nursery – be careful to avoid similarity with that of any other local nursery. Successful ones have included animals (eg squirrel, robin, frog), flowers (sunflower, daisy) and simple pictures of children. A line drawing is the best option, not a fussy picture.

How to advertise

You will have to decide which method or combination of methods suits you and your pocket best. Bear in mind that, as you are registered, you will appear on either or both of the local authority's social services and education lists, which is a big start. Gain permission for your own leaflets, posters or brochures to be left free in local libraries, surgeries, health clinics, drop-in centres and church noticeboards. Don't forget local parent and toddler groups or small magazines such as parish and the local branch of the National Childbirth Trust (NCT) – among the readers are tomorrow's clients. You can also ask your present clients to take a few leaflets and put them up in places they think of.

As you almost certainly have a limited budget, you need to concentrate on advertising that reaches the right target. Leaflet drops through letterboxes, for example, are expensive, look a bit desperate and are not likely to produce much result.

Local papers, on the other hand, often have a special supplement for nurseries and schools: an advertisement here may be a bit expensive, but more likely to produce results. If you can afford it, a regular monthly advertisement in the local press is a good reminder to people that you exist, and you may be able to negotiate a discount with the publisher. If you are serving a particular employer, union or group, it will

Depending on your nursery's name, you might find your own logo is a great marketing aid be in their interest to help you advertise through any in-house publication and they will often give you a very good deal.

Taking a listing in *Yellow pages* or other local directory is helpful and make sure that you are in the telephone directory under your correct name – not under a proprietor's, which is totally frustrating to any client looking you up.

For the adventurous, offering a display at a local exhibition or trade fair will put you on the map to a wider audience.

As for your current clients, you might consider asking them to complete a questionnaire to assess how well you are meeting their needs. This would not need to be done more than once a year; assuming children stay with you for two to three years, biannually is probably better.

> The best advertising is word of mouth from a satisfied customer. The grapevine is very powerful

Sample questionnaire to test parental satisfaction:
- How did you hear about us?
- What made you choose this nursery?
- Do you feel we keep you sufficiently well-informed about your child's progress?
- Do you find the staff:
  Approachable, friendly?
  Ready to give advice if this is needed?
  Knowledgeable about your child and his or her particular needs?
  Give the impression of professionalism?
  Respond satisfactorily to requests?
- Would you say your child was happy in nursery?
- Does he/she enjoy the nursery because:
  Relationships with staff are happy?
  Of the other children?
  The activities are enjoyable?
  The facilities meet his/her needs?
- Do you feel that the nursery consults you sufficiently about policy or policy changes?
- Do you think we offer good support to parents?
- Are there any things about which you are not happy?
- Are there any things we do not do which you would like us to do?

'Thank you for the time you have given to complete this questionnaire. We wish to provide as good a service as we can for parents and this must be one of the ways we can test opinions and ascertain the extent to which we can meet parents' needs and expectations.'

Remember the best form of advertising is word-of-mouth recommendation from a satisfied customer. Parents talk endlessly about education and educational establishments and are always seeking information from each other. The grapevine is very, very powerful. It takes a long time to build up a reputation but it can be lost overnight.

CHAPTER EIGHT:

Managing the environment

Management of the physical environment of the nursery has two components:
- That the environment is **child-friendly**, promotes a child's well-being and ability to thrive physically and to learn through play and structured activity.
- That the environment is **safe** and complies with the relevant parts of the Children Act 1989, the Health & Safety at Work Act 1974, the Food Safety Regulations 1995 and other relevant legislation as regulated by local authority officers.

Starting with the first point, it is useful to visit and observe other nurseries, to attempt to see through the eyes of a child and to imagine yourself at child height. You could perhaps discuss your own nursery with a trained designer or architect.

Case study: evaluation exercise
The staff of a London nursery began by listing the areas of basic provision that the nursery should contain. For each area, they then listed 'ideal features'. Taking an area at a time, they then tried to make the necessary changes so that each matched the standard they had set.

This was a lengthy exercise, but extremely worthwhile as it tapped staff professionalism and creativity, engaged the children and parents and resulted in a very well-ordered environment. It broke an apparently daunting task – re-assessing the physical layout and internal coherence of the different sectors of the nursery – down into manageable steps.

The staff first decided that the nursery should contain the following basic provision, in alphabetical order:

Book corner	Garden	Physical play (gross motor)
Computer	Home corner	Sand play (wet and dry)
Construction	Investigative area	Small world
Cooking	Malleable materials	Table top games
Craft, including woodwork	Music and sound	Water play
Dressing-up	Painting	

As an example, here are the features of their 'ideal' water play area:

- The vessel should be transparent so that children can observe from a wider range of angles, including from below.
- The water has shallow and deeper parts.
- The floor on which it stands is easily wiped and the surface is non-slip.
- Resources to use in the water tray are available for children to choose.
- Resources are stored in groups to comply with themes eg floating and sinking, absorbent materials, pouring, water wheels, Archimedian screw, capacity, etc.
- Resources include waterproof toys for imaginative play eg animals, figures, boats.
- Protective waterproof aprons and towels for children to dry their hands are hung close by.
- A maximum group of children should be established, though sometimes one child may choose to play alone there.
- It can be easily emptied by staff.

Each individual zone is obviously part of a wider whole. It would make no sense to site the water area too far away from the sinks for filling and emptying or too near the book or painting area, for obvious reasons.

At the end of the exercise, staff decided to continue to review each area on a regular basis. It would be subjected to a detailed observation procedure to assess uptake (how children gained from it) and equal opportunity issues and to identify further possible improvements.

THE ENVIRONMENT AND THE SENSES

Sound: Professionals should ask if sound levels in the nursery are too high. Children obviously need reasonable quiet in order to sleep. Constant noise is both over-stimulating and tiring for very young children (see *Babyhood*, Penelope Leach, 1974) even when they are awake. Noise activates auditory receptor nerves but babies and young children have not yet learned to screen out what they do not want or do not need to hear. Many workers with young children complain of their inability to listen: in a society beset with noise pollution they have become too confused by generalised noise, plus perhaps permanent television or music, to be selective.

Within the nursery, should be quiet areas to allow for rest and sleep, conversation, and reading. Soft furnishings and carpet absorb sound; hard floors and bare walls reflect it. Care should be taken to separate the noisy activities from quiet ones, not to zone them side by side.

Background colours should be neutral to provide calm and a good backdrop for displays

Sight: Background colours should be neutral to provide calm and a good backdrop for displays. Displays should be primarily of children's work. Too many nurseries get carried away with murals devised and executed by staff: striking, but too permanent and detrimental to children's creativity, especially if they reproduce commercial characters from television and films.

Displays should be changed regularly, relate to themes or topics which are under discussion and be at a height appropriate for children to see. But beware of too much paper on the wall in corridors and stairways, as this is a great spreader of fire (see section on fire precautions, below).

Children should be able to see what equipment is freely available for them, which has implications for the height and nature of storage spaces. Boxes should be clearly labelled as to their contents, both in words and, where practical, by fixing one piece of what is inside to the outside or by fixing a picture of the item.

Lighting should be neither too dim nor too bright and harsh. Lights should simulate daylight. Certain areas, eg reading, painting, may need more focused lighting or to be near natural daylight.

Care should be taken to separate quiet from noisy activities and wet/messy from clean/dry

Touch: A reasonable part of the nursery should be carpeted since children will carry out much of their activity on the floor and this provides a warm and comfortable surface and one which reduces injury from falls.

Similarly, as the nursery is a 'home' as well as a 'school', it needs lots of soft places where children can relax and be comfortable: big cushions, bean bags, sofas.

There should be a wide range of materials on offer for children to cook with. Paper and card of different textures, cloth of all types, wood of different sorts and strengths, metal, clay, dough, different types of art materials (different paints, felt-tips, wax crayons, wooden pencils, chalks) and anything else that you can think of. Toys and equipment should also reflect a variety of materials and reliance should not be placed on an overabundance of primary-coloured plastic.

MOVEMENT AND MOBILITY

There should be clearly defined areas for particular activities: children find this reassuring and staff more convenient. If materials can be stored near where they are needed there will be far less carting things around and children's independence will be fostered. There will have to be doubling up,
of course: the same tables will almost certainly be used for craft as for juice and biscuits and lunch, but the sand corner should remain the sand corner and the reading area the reading area.

'Pathways' between areas should enable people to move from one part of the nursery to another without interfering with activities that are taking place.

Care should be taken to separate quiet from more noisy activities and the wet/messy from the clean/dry.

There should be places where children can withdraw and rest when they feel the need.

The environment should be 'enabling' – ie permit children to move around freely and make their own choices.

MAINTENANCE

Obviously, working, painting, modelling children will make a mess. Wet, messy activities should be confined to washable, non-slip floor areas. Where children can safely help tidy up, they should be encouraged to do so and the old adage about tidying up before moving on to the next thing is vital: children learn and adults function better in an orderly environment.

Multi-piece items should be checked and counted before being put away. Use little tricks like numbering the back of each piece of a jigsaw with the same number to help keep sets complete and help with identification if any pieces do go astray.

The nursery should be cleaned regularly, over and above the clearing up after activities cleaning.

OUTDOORS

A large, empty space (if you are lucky enough to have one) is intimidating. Children appreciate 'features' and 'zones': a wooden 'boat', a set of low stepping stones, a place where older ones can play rudimentary ball games. Large, fixed equipment that can challenge children's physical and imaginative play is important, as are wheeled toys, suitable for individual and group use and small physical play equipment for practising co-ordination and sports skills: bats, balls, bean bags, hoops. An outdoor sandpit (covered) and water in the summer too, of course. Sometimes play will be free; at other times, directed to develop early gymnastic and group games skills.

All the activities you do can sometimes take place outside.

HEALTH AND SAFETY

It is legally and morally paramount to be vigilant with regards to the health and safety of the children in the care of the nursery. The person in charge must also be health and safety officer or appoint another person to this role. There should be a written health and safety policy document, copies of which should be given to all team members, students, trainees and helpers. Staff should make it their duty to educate children to begin to assume responsibility for their own health and safety, as a key part of the curriculum. In every respect, prevention is the watchword and correct reaction the second line of defence. The local authority watchdogs will make their checks, but the manager should be aware of the main planks of legislation (see above) and seek to act in the spirit of them. For example, there is nothing in the Food Safety (General Food Hygiene) Regulations to cover food that is not prepared on the premises, but it would be a careless nursery that allowed children's packed lunches, perhaps containing yoghurt and ham or chicken, to sit in the sun or near a radiator for several hours before consumption.

There should be a written health and safety policy, with copies given to all team members

SAFETY

Children must be supervised at all times. You will need to:

- Complete a register at the beginning of every session so that you know who is there. (This might be combined with a learning exercise for the children: instead of simply answering their name at register time, they could take their name, drawn on eg a Velcro-backed cardboard petal, and fix it to their name space on eg a flower on the register flowerbed on the wall. Young children could be assisted with this by a helper. Then a different child each day could help count the children and adults present to confirm numbers.)
- Keep that register in a known place.
- Ensure that all parents/carers, if they are not in their usual place, give you alternative numbers as a matter of course. Parents whose jobs involve regular travel outside the office/ home should be encouraged to consider a mobile phone.
- Make sure that if the group has access to separate yet connecting areas, including a garden, that each area has an adult assigned to it. They may move with the children elsewhere, but should check their 'own' area frequently. All adults should be aware of children going into the toilet(s).
- Provide extra-careful supervision for children at the water or sand trays or acquiring skills with tools such as scissors, hammers, junior hacksaws, pincers, screwdrivers etc. Staff should know the correct and safe way to use the tools, eg the way to use pincers to remove nails and select tools appropriate to the age group.
- A particular member of staff should have responsibility for checking premises for any hazardous or undesirable litter eg plastic bags, syringes, drinks cans and condoms, which may have been left by others in between sessions.

Outside the nursery

- Parental consent must be obtained in writing before any trips off the premises occur. A general one when children start nursery could cover trips to the local shops; separate ones should be presented for special trips further afield.
- Extra adults will be needed.
- Young children should wear reins when walking along roads.
- Make sure that a preliminary visit is made to assess potential difficulties or hazards so that a strategy can be worked out for dealing with them 'on the day'. The same visit should be used to ascertain position of toilets, first aid post, telephones if you do not carry a portable phone (should you?).
- If using staff or parents' cars, correct insurance cover must be taken. Seat belts and children's seats must be checked for correct fitting to the child's size/weight.
- Take water, sun cream and hats in summer; waterproof clothing as needed. Take first aid kit and list of parents' contact telephone numbers.
- Use the opportunity to increase children's awareness of traffic lights, pelican

crossings and road crossing drill as in the Green Cross Code.

Accident procedure

- You will need an accident report book kept in a known and accessible place. All accidents, whether involving children or adults, should be recorded in it. Pages should be ruled in the following way:

Date and time	Name	Nature of accident	Injury	Action taken	Witness/es

Parents should be informed of any accident involving their child that has been entered into the accident book. The book should be the subject of regular staff discussion to consider whether the accident could have been avoided and whether any practice should be altered to avoid re-occurrence.

- You may wish to require parents to sign a consent form enabling you to sign a hospital consent form in the event of an emergency.
- Minor accidents will need to be treated and details entered into the accident book. If a child needs hospital treatment you could:
  a) Call an ambulance.
  b) Take the child in a car driven by an insured member of staff. You will also need another adult in the car with her.
  c) Call a taxi.

If staff have to go off premises with a child, back-up staff or a parent from a rota system will need to be called in to the nursery. Make sure you have such a system in operation. In all cases parents must of course be informed as soon as possible.

First Aid

There should always be two qualified first-aiders on the premises as well as a comprehensive first aid book and kit. The first-aiders should have completed a course with specific reference to children. One must be nominated the named first aid officer and her name and location should be displayed in the nursery. The kit should be correctly labelled with a green cross on a white background and its contents checked regularly for replacement. It should be in a known and accessible place, but obviously out of the reach of children. Any drugs, medicines, inhalers etc that may be needed by children should be in a lockable cupboard but the key must be always accessible to staff.

There should be two qualified first-aiders on the premises plus a first aid book and kit

To help first-aiders, extract relevant medical information from children's registration forms and make medical reference cards to be kept in a card index box near the telephone (name and number of parent, GP, any allergic reactions, etc.).

Fire precautions

The fire service is not the licensing authority for nurseries: the social services department of the local authority is, but the fire service acts as the fire safety adviser and will assess the fire safety measures at the nursery. Social services will then inform the person in charge of the nursery what standards must be applied before a licence is granted. If a nursery is to be installed in work premises, however, which comes under the Fire Precautions Act (1971), an application will need to be made to the fire service for changes to the fire certificate.

Re-inspection requirements vary according to the local authority. You can ask your local fire service for advice if you are uncertain on any point. They probably publish specific guidelines for nurseries (the London Fire Brigade's Fire Safety Guidance Note Number 3 is *Fire precautions in nurseries and crèches*, for example). You should:

> In the event of a real fire, no child should ever be able to dash back to rescue a possession

- Ensure that nursery staff are trained in evacuation procedures and that everybody knows the correct exit(s) and assembly points – including parents who should go to the assembly points to find their children, not to the nursery.
- Hold regular fire drills (we recommend 12-weekly). The fire drill procedure should be written and posted on the wall of every room and by the telephone. You do not want to over-alarm children. Talking about fire drills and their purpose, making up or reading relevant stories, having a play fire station: all these will help children come to terms with their anxieties. In the event of a real fire, no child should ever be able to dash back in to rescue a possession or a pet; however, another way of calming children's anxieties about fire risk to nursery pets is to have a designated pet officer (an adult) whose job it is to take the animal with them as part of the fire drill.
- Ensure that extinguishers, fire blankets, smoke detectors, etc are in the best position, are in working order and are the right type – water would be dangerous on a fire involving fats and oils, for example. These must all be regularly checked and the inspection recorded.
- Ensure that passageways and exits are clear of furniture and equipment. Do not install children's or other work on paper along the main fire exit passageways: it is one of the best promoters of the spread of fire.
- Have flame-retardant upholstery and fabrics.
- Turn electrical equipment off after use.
- Ban smoking and have No Smoking notices posted.
- Appropriately guard all heaters.
- Have a cooker which does not require the use of matches.

Carbon monoxide precautions

Faulty central heating or gas fires can cause this silent and deadly danger. Ensure that there is natural ventilation and have carbon monoxide detectors (similar to smoke alarms) fitted. All heating systems should be checked at least annually.

SECURITY

Doors: External doors should have five-lever mortise deadlocks which conform to the current British Standard, a spy hole and door chain and security bolts for night time. A system of double doors enclosing a small vestibule is best for the main entrance. The inner door of this vestibule should have a handle above child height. French windows giving onto outside areas should have locks top and bottom and safety glass fitted.

Internal doors should have slow-closing mechanisms to prevent injured fingers. Toilet doors should not be lockable from the inside.

Windows: Any windows accessible by children should have childproof locks fastened and not be able to be opened more than a few inches. Any low windows should be fitted with safety glass.

Floors: Change or find some way of overcoming floor surfaces that are too slippery or become slippery in certain conditions eg when wet or sandy (these could be regularly mopped or swept). Use moisture control matting at the main door to reduce foot tread, pram or pushchair wheels, umbrellas and dripping clothes causing wet floors. Rugs should be firmly secured, but are better avoided.

Stairs: Stairgates must be fitted top and bottom (depending on the age of children on the premises). Bannisters/guard rails must be in good condition with no child size gaps. No open stair treads. Stair rail at an appropriate height, on the wall side as well as the opposite side. Stair carpets must be checked regularly to make sure the treads are firmly fixed.

Heating/hot water: Heating and ventilating systems must work correctly to provide the legally minimum temperature of 65° - 70°F (18° - 21°C) for babies. Hot water must be thermostatically controlled so children do not burn hands while washing. All fires/radiators must be appropriately guarded.

Kitchen: Children should not normally be allowed in this area. Fit a door gate or stable door. See fire precautions, above, and avoid deep frying. Adults should consume hot drinks away from children. Children eating must be seated and supervised: choking or slipping on dropped food are dangers.

Storage: There should be no unstable storage (shelves, cupboards, filing cabinets). Some become unstable if all drawers are pulled out. Make sure all storage areas are kept tidy with no trip hazards. Storage for eg cleaning materials must be child secure and preferably in an area such as the kitchen which is normally out-of-bounds to children. Children's equipment which is used only under supervision (eg scissors, tools) should be locked away when not in use.

Electrical equipment: This should be inspected regularly for safe condition, eg casing, connection of lead to casing, having an integral plug, sound lead insulation and correct fuse in plug. Fit short, curly flexes wherever possible and avoid all extension or other trailing leads. Earth integrity test at least annually. Include any electrical equipment brought from home by staff/parents before it is used in nursery.

Switch off and unplug all electrical equipment after use. Fit all electrical sockets with blanking devices. Make sure the children cannot get near any electrical apparatus.

Fit short, curly flexes wherever possible and avoid all extension or other trailing leads

Equipment: No child under three should have access to small items which could represent a choking hazard. But three- and four-year-olds will need to use small equipment and toys as part of their curriculum. Ensure separate storage and access.

Ensure that all toys are painted with 'pica' risk low lead paint. Avoid glass equipment. There is almost always a plastic equivalent. Avoid equipment that is hinged dangerously or splintered.

Outside: Is the play area secure? The minimum height for a fence should be 120 cm (4 feet), with no gaps beneath and ideally made of chain link. Are walls in a good condition? Any access gates or doors must have strong security locks. Make sure that cars and car parking do not intrude on the play area.

Clean the sand pit regularly and cover when not in use. Check area daily in case dogs or cats have made messes. Clear these away before use. Check that all pipe and drain covers are safe. Check section on living things (below) to ensure that there are no poisonous plants in or overhanging your play area.

Outside play equipment: Inspect this weekly for its safety and condition; make sure any bolts are adequately tight. Do not allow children to use climbing equipment when wearing trailing scarves, belts, flapping coats, flip-flops or footwear with slippery or high-heeled soles. Do not use climbing frames in wet weather.

Ensure that there are adequate safety surfaces beneath equipment to absorb the shock of impact. If you have chosen bark, ensure that it is 'topped up' to a sufficient depth.

Water: Any pond must be covered with a fixed frame with rigid mesh grille (mesh size must not exceed 150 cm or six inches) or with a 120 cm (4 feet) high fence. If the pond backs on to a neighbour's land, the dividing fence should be childproof.

HEALTH

Illness

You should have a published policy on exclusion when children are unwell. Your local health centre will have advice regarding times of exclusion for the usual childhood infections; here is a brief guide:

Illness and incubation period (days)	Period when infectious	Minimum period of exclusion
Chickenpox 11-21	1 day before to 6 days after appearance of rash	6 days from onset of rash
Rubella (German measles) 14-21	Few days before to 4 days after onset of rash	4 days from onset of rash (avoid/warn women under 14 weeks' pregnant)
Measles 10-15	Few days before to 5 days after onset of rash	7 days from onset of rash
Mumps 12-26 (commonly 18)	Few days before to subsidence of swelling	Until swelling has gone
Whooping cough (pertussis) 7-10	From 7 days after exposure to 21 days after onset of paroxysmal cough	21 days from onset of paroxysmal cough

The exclusion period for skin infections is: until treatment has been received for cases of pediculosis and scabies and until the spots have healed in cases of impetigo.

Your registration form will indicate whether the children have had routine immunisation. If they have not, ask why – there may have been contra-indications or the parent may have chosen not to immunise, but there is always the possibility that they have simply overlooked vaccination (a recent study in Cleveland found that two thirds of parents of young children who had missed at least one routine vaccination thought that the children were fully immunised even though they had been sent as many as nine reminders that they were not).

Your feelings on exclusion may vary, but it is unfair to expose other children or adults unnecessarily to the risk of illness, which may in some cases affect the running of the nursery.

Here is one nursery's published sickness policy:
- When a child becomes ill at nursery every effort will be made to contact the parents, who will be requested to collect their child as soon as possible.
- In most cases when a child is sent home we feel it would be beneficial for them to see a doctor.
- Please notify us if you are aware your child has a contagious illness or if the cause of the illness has been confirmed by a doctor.
- Children suffering from sickness or diarrhoea must not return to nursery until at least 24 hours have elapsed from the last bout of sickness/diarrhoea and they are eating normally.

I the undersigned have read and agree to the above policy.

You will need to work out how you will comfort and care for children who become sick while at nursery while waiting for their parents to take them home.

You will also need to discuss procedures with parents of children who require daily medication or for their condition to be monitored (eg diabetes) or who suffer dangerous reactions to eg nuts or bee/wasp stings. You will have to ensure that the nursing skills of staff adequately match the illness or condition of any child attending nursery.

HYGIENE

- Give routine advice to parents about dealing with head lice and threadworm.
- Establish routines for children to wash their hands after going to the toilet and before meals.
- When children have their own named washcloth and towel on their own pegs these must be washed weekly. Discourage children from using anyone else's.
- You must be aware of the latest advice in relation to managing children who are HIV-positive; in particular, in relation to dealing with body spillages (blood, faeces, vomit) and ensure that you have the relevant facilities and equipment. Body spillages should be dealt with in this manner, for the safety of all, whether you know you have a confirmed HIV-positive child on the premises or not.

Cooking: The importance of hygiene in cooking is such that anyone preparing food on the premises may be deemed by the local Environmental Health service to require a food and hygiene certificate and the kitchen and food serving areas/methods will themselves be inspected by the local Environmental Health service.

The main dangers, assuming that there is cleanliness of the kitchen and of hands which touch the food, are from the temperature at which food is kept and served (too warm and dangerous bacteria will breed to too high a level) and from salmonella in undercooked eggs. All refrigerators should operate at a temperature of 5° C (41° F) or lower, freezers – 15° C (5° F). Keep a thermometer in each. Food to be served hot should be kept at or above a temperature of 63° C (obviously it will need a cooling time when served to avoid burns). Only cook food from frozen if recommended to do so by the manufacturer. If there is a power cut for three hours or longer, check that food is still frozen and use any thawed food immediately.

The details of the Food Safety Act 1995 are in a booklet (G21/007 3002 1P 200k July 95) available from the Department of Health and in a leaflet from Eaton Publications (01932 229001).

As cooking and serving meat poses all kinds of hazards, special must be taken. Children bringing their own packed lunches is an option that is less trouble in some ways for the nursery, but packed lunch boxes need to be kept cold, particularly if there are meat or dairy products inside.

All raw fruit and vegetables should be thoroughly washed. Carrots should be peeled. All manner of food advisory guidelines may be instituted depending on current research: nursery managers should pay close attention to the advice issued by the Department of Health via local authority environmental health departments.

Parents should have let you know of any dietary restrictions, food reactions or allergies suffered by their child. You must be aware of these when preparing and serving food. The main ones will be to cow's milk (Between 0.5 per cent and 0.1 per cent of people cannot tolerate cow's milk), eggs, wheat or fish, but there are many others and they appear to be increasing. Perhaps the most deadly is an allergy to nuts, in particular, peanuts: even a tiny trace can kill once a person is sensitised. Most nurseries will be aware that peanuts are not safe for children under five, but any child might have peanut butter sandwiches in a lunch box, some foods contain chopped nuts – very close advice needs to be taken on this and many other food issues and it is the the nursery manager's job to ensure that it has been.

Cooking with children is an important part of the curriculum. For safety's sake this tends to avoid boiling, frying and cutting, but too often it is simply preparation of sugary foods. Cooking sessions should set an example by avoiding too much sugar, salt and fat and should contain talk about the importance of fresh fruit and vegetables and the avoidance of processed food. Keep a balance of savoury and sweet.

Cooking sessions should set a good example by avoiding too much sugar, salt and fat

Living things: Keeping animals and plants, even for a short time, helps children develop a sense of responsibility and develops nurturing. However, it must be under close adult supervision.

● The nature of small mammals – their rapid movement, unpredictability and their instinctive terror – makes them difficult to handle with care and judgement required. Children therefore should not hold them. They can be brought to the group in containers which make observation easy. Adults can use the opportunity to demonstrate careful handling with a commentary that directs attention to the characteristics of the animal and encourages empathy.

- Cages must be kept scrupulously clean and need to be of such a design that this is possible.
- Fish and mini-beasts such as worms, woodlice, snails, slugs and stick insects make excellent creatures for close observation. Aquariums need good electrical/RCD protection.
- The decreasing variety of amphibia means that frogs and toads and their spawn are best left in ponds. The provision of a pond in an outdoor area is therefore of great value for conservation as well as for observation by children, but they are a great danger (see above for safety advice).
- Providing wild birds with food, water and nesting boxes where appropriate is particularly suitable for promoting a caring attitude.
- Children should be encouraged to grow and study plants. They should be warned never to eat berries growing in the wild and to be careful of thorns and stinging nettles. Beware of roses and other prickly plants in a children's garden.
- The following common plants are highly poisonous and staff must be aware of the dangers they present:

    Daffodil and other bulbs; all parts of the potato plant (except the actual potato tuber) and tomato plant (except the tomato fruit); rhubarb leaves; cuckoo pint; yew; black, deadly and woody nightshade; white and black bryony; hemlock; henbane; ragwort; holly; mistletoe; giant hogweed; laburnum; mountain ash berries; privet; horse chestnuts (conkers).

- Dead animals should never be examined by children in your care. Old nests and feathers should only be examined through plastic bags.

Keeping animals and plants, even for a short time, helps children develop a sense of nurturing

CHAPTER NINE

Managing the curriculum

Overseeing the programme of activities designed for the children in the nursery is obviously an important managerial function. The quality of the direction given will have a very significant impact on the knowledge, concepts, skills and attitudes which children acquire while they are there and is likely to have an important effect on their education in the future. The quality of the curriculum will undoubtedly affect children's happiness in nursery and parental perceptions about its value for their child.

For any supplier of care and education for four-year-olds who hopes to register as a 'provider' under the Department for Education and Employment's nursery voucher scheme, the curriculum will have to encompass achieving the goals that have been gathered under the heading 'Desirable outcomes for children's learning on entering compulsory education', ie by the term after their fifth birthday (see Appendix four). It would be a poor curriculum that did the minimum in this respect, however; that, for example, drilled children to write their own names in upper and lower case letters, and then put writing instruments and paper away.

In this chapter, babies, toddlers and three-to-five-year-olds are described separately and it is assumed that they will have their own areas or rooms. However, there are many times during the day when it will be beneficial for all age groups to mingle: the younger ones will be entertained by and learn from the example of older children while the latter will benefit from the chance to learn and practise interaction with younger children. Being all together for at least some playtimes and meals, for example, will promote a family atmosphere within a nursery.

A CURRICULUM FOR BABIES

Curriculum might seem a rather grandiose word and its application to children before their first birthday somewhat pretentious. However, as it simply means the activities and experiences which we plan and which children initiate for themselves, it is perfectly reasonable to consider it in relation to babies.

At this age, our greatest concern, as caring adults, must be to make the baby feel loved and emotionally secure. This places a major responsibility on the key worker who needs to be knowledgeable, sensitive and responsive when dealing with the needs, moods and feelings of the child.

Piaget, the great developmental psychologist, called the first two years of life the sensori-motor phase and the curriculum for the first year therefore needs to be planned so that it builds upon the individual baby's stage of physical development and compulsion to use his senses in order to explore and conceptualise. The adult's role is to select and offer as many appropriate, safe, enjoyable and learning experiences as possible.

Important milestones are reached during the first year of life. It is therefore vital for those designing the curriculum to:

- Have a thorough knowledge of child development. (An essential book is *From birth to five years: Children's developmental progress* by Mary D Sheridan, NFER Publishing 1973 and Routledge 1992)

- Observe individual children to match their particular milestones against what can be expected, allowing for normal variations.

- Recognise that children need lots of opportunities to consolidate new knowledge and skills.

- Simultaneously remember that children are naturally curious and pre-disposed to respond enthusiastically to new experiences, so variety and novelty are extremely important.

- Be able to use language to interact with the baby and to label, comment and explain about objects and activities within the baby's sphere. From the moment of birth, the baby should be hearing lots of language, much of which should be directed specifically towards the baby.

- Understand that during the sensori-motor phase, the physical, intellectual, social and emotional aspects of learning are inextricably linked.

> It is vital to recognise that children need the chance to consolidate new knowledge and skills

Case study

In the baby room at a local community nursery serving working parents, the manager, Irene, asked staff to consider structuring a programme based on the five senses. What they came up with is detailed and reflects a great deal of thought. Their format, which can be used to structure work based on any of the five senses, is offered below:

- What experiences can be provided to stimulate and thus develop the sense in question?
- List the resources that will be needed.
- The accompanying language and non-verbal communication.
- The setting for the activity.
- Monitoring time, duration, frequency and quality of interactions.
- Observing and recording childís responses and reporting to parents.
- Deciding on next stages.

Here is their planning for the sense of **touch**. Readers may care to use it in helping them shape schedules of work on the other senses.

Experiences

- The nature of the fabrics the child feels in clothing, bedding, surfaces, toys and care routine settings. Carers' clothing, soft furnishings, etc. All of these fabrics should represent a wide range from the natural and synthetic worlds.
- The nature of the objects they handle (and put in their mouth). Here, safety must be the adult's first consideration. Thereafter, there is a multiplicity of toys made from varied materials, household objects, artefacts, natural items etc for the baby to explore. Within these, staff need to make sure that a wide range of physical properties are presented, to include:

Matt/shiny, flexible/rigid, soft/hard, light/heavy, compressible/resistant, warm to touch/cold to touch, sound producing/sound absorbing, transparent/opaque, rough/smooth. All colours and shapes.

The way such experiences are presented to children is important. It means preparation beforehand in play where children are discovering things for themselves. Readers may, for example, be aware of the treasure basket idea presented by Elinor Goldschmied and Sonia Jackson (*People under three*, Routledge, 1994). Here, children are offered a simple basket with no handles, with fairly shallow sides, in which there are a variety of natural objects from which they can select and explore. Often, two sitting babies are placed opposite one another and they both select items from the same basket.

There are, of course, other means of enabling children to enjoy such heuristic play eg cardboard 'cupboards', bags, lidded vessels. Such activities almost invariably absorb them for long periods of time and aid their developing powers of concentration.

- Physical contact – cuddling, affectionate comfort touching, stroking, play touching, clapping hands etc as well as body massage provided by the carer. Accepting the baby's natural inclination to touch the carer. All these have important implications for the baby's sense of well-being as well as providing sensory information.
- Care routines offer many opportunities for babies to explore their physical environment through touch. At mealtimes they will handle their food with its variety of textures. For this reason, the sooner they can feed themselves, the better. At bathtime they will enjoy all the pleasure that warm water offers as well as learning about the unique quality of liquids. They will experience the special textures of sponge or flannel and the way things become slippery when soap is applied.

Resources, language and setting

The resourcing, accompanying language and settings are all implied within the experiences listed and Irene was keen to ensure that staff appreciated the complexity and potential of the programmes.

Monitoring, observing, recording and reporting

Here, Irene is keen to monitor the quality of the interaction between adults and children and the resultant learning which takes place. Moreover, she insists that staff observe the children's responses to the activities provided and that they record significant developments which can then be communicated to parents.

Progression

Finally, Irene asked staff to say what they would provide next for individuals in the light of their observations. To help in this process, she suggested staff repeat their use of their original seven headings.

To sum up, a quality baby curriculum will demand that adults respond and interact lovingly with children both during care routines, at other times and during 'playtimes'.

Provide frequent chances in the nursery for babies to exercise in an age appropriate manner

- Plan for games like peek-a-boo, hiding and finding things, contact play like 'Round and round the garden' and eg 'This little piggy' at appropriate times.
- Recognise that adult talk will feature prominently and that prelanguage 'conversations' in sound will also take place.
- Make sure that books will be presented to babies as soon as they can sit up.
- Provide frequent opportunities for babies to exercise within the environment in a way appropriate to their stage of development.
- Ensure that adults will support the child's attempts to reach 'milestones' such as rolling over, sitting up, standing, crawling, 'cruising' and walking.
- Make heuristic (self-discovery) play experiences part of the curriculum as soon as the child can enjoy them.
- Make music, rhyme and song feature prominently in each baby's day.

A CURRICULUM FOR TODDLERS

This will include planning for 'areas of learning'. The main ones are:

The social/moral	**The imaginative**	**The creative**
The linguistic	**The investigative and exploratory**	**The physical**

The manager will need to be certain that those in charge of toddlers are knowledgeable and experienced in providing for all these inter-connected areas of learning. In order to do this, she herself will need to be reasonably familiar with child development at this age. Taking just one area of the six listed as an example, the **social/moral**, consider the many facets that the nursery needs to provide for:

Organisation of the physical environment
- There should be enough equipment and enough for any one type of activity to avoid children becoming frustrated – no point in having just one spade in the sandpit or only one engine with the train layout.
- A quantity of toys and equipment need to be of a type – eg large scale, floor-based – which promote socialisation.
- Care must be taken to determine a group size which is appropriate to the nature of the activity on offer. This will vary according to the ability and developmental stage of the children and also needs to be considered with respect to safety and to ensure that the children can interact effectively with the activity. For painting, for example, each child requires an individual supply of paper, brushes, paint and enough space. Cookery demands one adult to a group of two/three children depending on the children and the recipe. Music-making could be done in a group of about six, perhaps with another adult.
- There should be features which draw upon children's natural inclination to nurture: eg plants to be tended, bird tables, nesting boxes and toys which, by their very nature, encourage caring behaviour. Dolls should be 'babies' capable of being cuddled, bathed and taken for walks. In nurseries with babies, there should be times when they mingle so that toddlers become aware of the different way in which babies need to be cared for and learn, by example, to show them the correct consideration, to touch them gently, talk to them and 'help' them. The babies will benefit from the example of the older ones who in turn will benefit by having an opportunity to 'care for' younger ones.

The role of the adult
Adults should act as appropriate role models, demonstrating a co-operative, polite, kind and caring attitude towards other staff as well as children. Children should see that staff work as a team.

Adults should use language to comment on social behaviour and moral issues (at this stage, this will largely be to do with sharing, snatching, physical attacks such as pushing, biting, hair-pulling etc). They should explain behaviour codes and encourage empathy. Importantly, through modelling the strategy themselves, they should encourage children to think things through before they act.

> There should be a variety of features which draw upon children's natural inclination to nurture

'We bear in mind the individual child's age and understanding. Under two, if they snatch a toy, we intervene: "No, no, we don't snatch, let's find another one," or, "Let's ask for it when he's finished playing with it." We give the toy back gently and try to divert their play. With an older child, we say, "That wasn't very nice, shall we give it back?" and ensure that she returns the item and apologises. Then we praise her for doing so. If she continued not to be sociable, we would take her to play with something else for five minutes. If she went into a paddy, we would calm her down, then talk to her reasonably about it, so she understands why she was excluded from the activity.

'We try never to yell at a child across a room. It's more constructive to talk to them on a one-to-one basis.'

Syan, supervisor of a college nursery

Children should be made aware of how adults' work contributes to our society

- Adults should praise children whenever they show kindness to one another, to adults or to other living things or property.
- Adults should devise, communicate and maintain consistently a realistic behaviour policy. For example, try to let children finish talking before you interrupt, say, 'Excuse me' and 'Sorry' to them as you would expect them to say it to you.

Experiences which promote this learning

- Children should begin to be made aware of how adults' work contributes to the commonwealth of our society by looking at the work of those who directly help them eg mummy, daddy, the nursery cook.
- Stories should be told to children where good triumphs over evil. Many simple fairy and folk tales have value because of their optimistic message for small children who can, at times, feel overwhelmed by the seeming power of adults.
- Simple pretence situations with dolls, teddies and a range of props can be set up. Adults can either stand back and observe or participate in 'looking after' them. Other pretence is endless: toddlers enjoy 'making' adults meals/cups of tea, playing being doctors or nurses helping patients and acting out scenes from books.
- The enormous potential of mealtimes for creating an ethos for sharing and turn-taking should be fully exploited. There is no finer opportunity for the adult who sits with the children at table to be able to model and encourage socially desirable behaviour.
- Adults should bear in mind the importance of their tone of voice: pleasant at all times, albeit firm at some.

As many facets will need to be considered for the other five areas of a toddler curriculum. Taking an overall view, a quality toddler curriculum will need to:

- Recognise the child's need to be physically active. Ensure that maximum use is made of the nursery garden and the wider world beyond (see chapter eight). Continue to help with physical milestones eg jumping, learning to balance.

- Capitalise on the normal rapid growth in language competence through the provision of good adult language modelling and presenting the relevant vocabulary to accompany new experiences. Ensure that books and literature feature prominently in the day. Ensure ample opportunity to have conversations with children.
- Ensure music and singing take place frequently.
- As children begin to acquire language they progress from simple imitative behaviour to actually pretending. There must therefore be ample opportunities for pretence and an ample supply of props and dressing-up clothes to pretend with. Adults must be prepared to join in where appropriate. They must also provide opportunities for the children to see and participate in activities which adults carry out to enable the maturing of imitative behaviour.
- Provide activities to foster the toddler's increasing desire to do things for him/ herself. Have a mixture of child-chosen and adult-led activities. Ensure that heuristic play continues; that children's natural curiosity is stimulated and satisfied. Allow and encourage experimentation.
- Enable children to express themselves through the arts and provide opportunities for fine manipulation.
- Help children to begin to understand the importance of caring and sharing and help support the child's natural desire to nurture. Foster children's positive self-image through support, encouragement and constructive criticism.
- Ensure that a balance exists between the security of the familiar and the stimulation of the new.

A CURRICULUM FOR THREE-TO-FIVE-YEAR-OLDS

Young children primarily learn through play, particularly when they feel safe and secure in supportive surroundings. Play must, however, be planned and purposeful and take into account the social, emotional, physical and intellectual aspects of this age group. 'Play' should not mean that children are not stretched and challenged or that they may not take an interest in early reading, writing and numeracy skills. Planning should take into account the needs of individual children and ensure that a policy of equal opportunities with regard to gender, race and special educational needs is addressed.

The adult role is essential: to plan the curriculum, to know how and when to interact and intervene, to extend children's vocabulary, to pose open-ended questions to make them think, to encourage problem-solving and to make observations and records of each child's development.

The curriculum outlined here should ensure that all these objectives are met. It will also meet even more than the desirable outcomes for children's learning as proposed in the Schools Curriculum and Advisory Service (SCAA) document on preschool education 1995, and so in turn will link with the National Curriculum Key Stage 1.

> Young children primarily learn through play, particularly when they feel safe and secure

Adults will find it helpful for children to have a theme upon which planning can be based and to make sure that all areas of the nursery are used effectively in the development of that theme. Themes can last for different periods of time; a term for one which will be explored from many different angles.

The theme can be applied to the various areas of learning – personal and social development, language and literacy, mathematics, knowledge and understanding of the world, physical development, creative development.

For example, one nursery chose **Houses and homes** as its topic one Spring term:

Week one: Settling in (this was actually a three-day week as nursery returned on a Wednesday).

Week two: New children, colours, sorting and matching, making patterns.

Weeks three and four: Storybook cottage, focusing on 'house' stories such as Three little pigs, Three bears, Red riding hood and Hansel and Gretel. This linked in with maths (numbers and counting); knowledge and understanding of the world (materials and their behaviour: what would make a strong house? Producing a design, helping to construct, co-operating in a group, understanding hard/soft, strong/weak, bendy/inflexible); language and literacy (can they retell a fairytale, predict what will happen next in a story, put events in sequence?).

Weeks five and six: Castles. This linked in with language and literacy (Sleeping Beauty, Jack and the Beanstalk, Cinderella, *The paperbag princess*, King Arthur, Robin Hood etc; retelling stories using puppets, oldest group presenting their own storybook, with help); knowledge and understanding of the world (looking at how castles differ from houses today, what features make a castle, can we build a similar structure, with drawbridge, moat, ramparts?); social skills (working in a group); and maths (shapes we see in a castle and concepts such as up/down, straight/curving).

This took the group to the half-term point with plenty to do (houses in miniature, houses near water, animal homes, our own homes) in the remainder of the term. There were trips and events such as walking around the locality looking at different types of houses, a visit to a building site, a visit to the canal to see boat homes. Cookery produced a cottage loaf and stained glass window biscuits. Outside, children built dens using different materials and looked for animal homes in the garden (worms, beetles, caterpillars, etc). In music and movement, the children learnt building songs and acted out the story of Three little pigs.

Clear sheets, explaining the theme, its associated activities and aims were photocopied and distributed to parents, divided by week and by sector of learning.

Personal and social development

An ethos should be created in the nursery whereby children relate happily with adults and with each other, through example, opportunity and discussion, learning to respect others and co-operate with them. From these contacts, children will be able to learn about their own personal history, their place in society and their local environment.

Language and literacy

Staff must be aware of the supreme importance of discussion in developing children's language competence. The nursery must therefore make speaking and listening an integral part of all activities. A wide variety of stories, poems, rhymes and songs should be presented and children should be encouraged to commit some of these to memory – because, of course, children thrive on the reassurance of repetition and ritual and hearing old favourites frequently will serve to consolidate vocabulary and memory. A rich story will have many levels to appreciate and inspire many different topics of conversation.

The book corner and storytelling time should feature prominently so that children come to love books, learn how to use them appropriately and want to learn to read. We must encourage children to understand that print conveys meaning by sharing books with them, labelling their work, displays and resources and drawing their attention to print all around them. As education researcher Professor Barbara Tizard and her co-authors wrote in *Young children at school in the inner city* (Lawrence Erlbaum, 1988), 'Simply introducing children to books in a happy atmosphere does not ensure that they will make a connection between meaning and print, or have any understanding of the written language.' Tricia David in *Under five – under educated*? (1990) suggests: 'Directing children's attentions to aspects of print, writing and so on, during activities, such as sharing a book, writing a shopping list together, disembeds that knowledge for the child and makes it accessible.'

Opportunities must always exist for children to make marks on paper, drawing, scribbling and eventually learning to write some letters accurately. Children need to learn to convey messages.

Staff must be aware of their role as models for children's language. It is therefore vital that consideration be given to the quality of explanation and instruction offered. A good deal of research has gone on in under-fives groups to assess how much adults talk to children and how helpful it is. It is a big subject, but it is clear that:

- Adults talking to younger children need to talk their way through what they are doing and need never be afraid to repeat themselves.

- 'Adults who offer older children lots of their own personal views, ideas and observations receive the child's views back in return. Those who ask lots of questions tend to get answers but little more. The more an adult questions a child, the less likely he is to elaborate on his answers, to take double turns or to ask questions of his own.' (*Working with under fives*, Oxford Preschool Research Project by David Wood, Linnet McMahon and Yvonne Cranstoun, Grant McIntyre, 1980)

> The book corner and storytelling should feature prominently so that children come to love books

- It is perfectly possible for adults never to listen children properly (watch out for automatic responses such as 'yes dear', 'really?' and 'that's nice') and to talk to them chiefly about mundane administration – 'Put on an apron', 'Go and wash your hands', 'Not so much noise please'.
- Activities of all sorts continue for longer and are generally more challenging and rewarding when an adult is present or involved.

The manager needs to be aware of the research findings relating to the area of conversation, talk and instruction and to transfer her knowledge to her staff. She needs to monitor the quality of the talk in her nursery so that it broadens the children's horizons, transfers knowledge and experience to them and enables them to talk fluently and confidently.

Physical development
Gross motor: Opportunities should exist for children to run, jump, climb and balance and to use a variety of small apparatus for throwing, catching, rolling, pushing, pulling, etc. The nursery should also make time for specific mime and movement sessions which link very well with music and sound.

Fine motor: Children should have an opportunity to use a wide range of tools and equipment and be able to handle many kinds of material.

Mathematics
Provide an extensive range of items to enable children to sort, classify, match, order and count.

Children should be able to handle and discuss a range of two- and three-dimensional shapes. Staff should be helping children to acquire the language of comparison eg 'taller than', 'lighter than/heavier than', 'larger than/smaller than'. They should also be helping children to use the language of spatial relationships. Such words as 'on', 'under', 'above', 'below', 'turn over' and 'turn round' should become part of their vocabulary in the activities they pursue.

Knowledge and understanding of the world
Opportunities should abound for children to observe the natural world at first hand, using their senses. They should be encouraged to describe and discuss what they see and to notice similarities and differences. We need to encourage children to question why things happen and say how they think things work.

Simple experiments, carefully supervised, can be designed to use the scientific method which involves observation, prediction, experimentation and communicating a conclusion eg drying the washing in different situations or freezing water then placing the ice in different situations to compare melt times.

Children should have the freedom to make things in order to solve the many problems that present themselves. It is therefore necessary to provide a wide range of tools and materials for the children to choose from and to talk with them about simple principles such as hinging, joining etc.

You should present collections of items from the man-made world eg different spoons, brushes or footwear, so that children can discuss what materials such things are made of and why.

Under close supervision, children should also be encouraged to use established and new technology – tape recorders, videos and the computer if you have one. Again, it is important for them to talk about their experiences with such things.

Creative development

Staff must plan for children to use a wide variety of ways including drawing, collage, painting, modelling in malleable materials, making models with waste materials, using construction kits and blocks or making a large-scale environment eg a space rocket or boat in which they can actually play. There should be opportunities for role play, drama/mime, dance and music and they should be encouraged to express themselves. They should have simple techniques demonstrated to them and be given opportunity to practise and perfect them.

> It is necessary to provide a wide range of different tools and materials to choose from

Outdoors

Everything which can be done indoors can usually be done outdoors. This is particularly important to remember in daycare, where children are in danger of missing out on the informal errands and excursions that their peers who stay at home more enjoy as a matter of course. Staff should plan to use the nursery garden and locality when planning work in each area of the curriculum.

It is in the garden that children have opportunities to study the natural world at first hand. They can learn about the rhythms and patterns of the seasons, about small living creatures and plants. The garden also presents physical challenges (see chapter eight), space to develop games and gymnastic skills and the necessity of sharing and turn-taking with such items as bikes.

Children should have their attention drawn to the work people do in the locality. Features such as different buildings, methods of transport and the changing landscape should be pointed out.

If the advice presented here is considered carefully and staff read widely about educational theory, keep abreast of current developments by reading professional literature and improve their practice by going on courses, there should be very little to be concerned about when the nursery is inspected for its quality of provision.

CHAPTER TEN:

Working with parents and the community

'You can't work in professional isolation – there is a world of contacts you need to be talking to, some close like your parents, others you only come across occasionally, like, for instance, people at the local library.'

Patricia (manager of a nursery attached to a college)

When Patricia became manager, she was very keen to put her nursery 'on the map'. She drew a simple web diagram and then set about considering how she would work with all the groups.

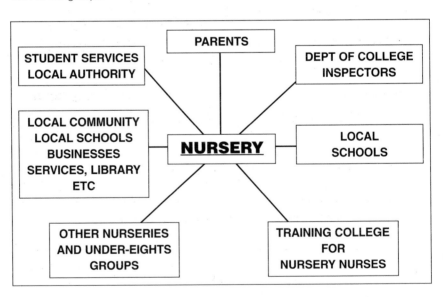

There are considerable advantages to a nursery in adopting an openly sociable and positive relationship policy. As the relationship with parents is the most important, both directly, in that you will work with their children and indirectly in that they will (or won't) recommend you to other parents, they form a natural starting point.

Parents should:

- Have open access to the nursery at any time.
- Be invited to exchange information about their child with a trusted adult (key worker) who knows him well and be able to contribute to their children's records.
- Feel free to seek advice from nursery staff.
- Be consulted on policy and policy changes.
- Have an elected representative, able to join relevant meetings.
- Participate in fund raising/social events.
- Be invited to 'evenings of interest' concerning child care/education.
- Perhaps have a **partnership agreement** like this, devised by Patricia. It highlights the roles and responsibilities of both parents and nursery staff and aims at promoting mutual understanding. It begins with an opening letter:

> Dear
> Everybody at Littlebears Nursery welcomes you and (child's name). We hope that, together, we can make (child's name) time here happy, safe and secure. We aim to meet children's educational needs through a carefully planned curriculum.
>
> In order that we can work in partnership, we ask you to enter into the following agreement. We undertake to make every effort to abide by its terms and ask you to do so as well.

LITTLEBEARS NURSERY 'PARENTS IN PARTNERSHIP' AGREEMENT	
NURSERY STAFF UNDERTAKE TO	**PARENTS AGREE TO**
Allow for a settling-in time. The length required for this depends on the individual child. We find this involves at least three sessions.	Attend nursery with their child during this settling-in time until he or she is happy to be left.
Provide 'open house' nursery and you are welcome at any time.	Open house policy.
Maintain a daily attendance register and record reasons for absence.	Inform us of any reasons for absences.
Not allow anyone except you or a person authorised by you to take your child home.	Inform us if they cannot collect their child and tell us who will do so on their behalf.

Parents should be invited to exchange information about their child with a trusted adult (key worker)

NURSERY STAFF UNDERTAKE TO	PARENTS AGREE TO
Plan a programme of activities to meet your child's individual needs, based on recorded observation.	Share their children's interests by talking with them about what they have been doing in nursery.
Keep a contact register in case you are unavailable.	Give us the names and telephone numbers of people we can contact in case of sickness or emergency and inform us of any changes.
Administer medicines prescribed by the doctor.	Give us written authorization to do this.
Do our best to comfort children who become ill during the day and we will inform you as soon as necessary.	Keep a sick child at home and collect one who becomes ill from nursery as soon as possible.
Advise you of any outbreaks of infections, diseases or cases of head lice.	Inform us if their child has contracted an infectious disease or has head lice.
Tell of any incidents in nursery which may have affected your child during the day.	Tell us of any significant happenings at home which may affect a child's behaviour in nursery.
Hold regular progress meetings where we provide you with an update on your child's progress – based on our records.	Tell us about their own observations and provide comments which can then be added to the child's record
Implement a policy of equal opportunities (enshrined in law). We help children learn about other cultures and aim to develop their respect and tolerance for race and religion. Boys and girls are treated equally and given equal access to all activities and appropriate responsibilities.	Accept the policy of equal opportunities within the nursery.

NURSERY STAFF UNDERTAKE TO	PARENTS AGREE TO
Keep a number of written policies in nursery including: **Equal Opportunities Behaviour Children's records**	Look at or have copies of these policies if they wish.
Provide a place for an elected parent representative on the nursery steering committee.	Either vote or possibly stand for election themselves.
Give you a monthly newsletter about the events and plans we have in mind for your children.	Read this and perhaps contribute comments/letters/articles.
Welcome feedback – both positive and negative if we are to monitor the service we provide	Discuss or write comments on what we are providing whenever they feel prompted or requested to do so.
Encourage your child to experiment with a variety of materials and be creative. In doing this they may get messy – even though we insist on aprons!	Provide sensible clothing for busy babies/toddlers/preschoolers.
Organise visits into the locality. We always advise you when this is planned.	Give their consent for this to happen.
Put on 'evenings of Interest' for parents.	Attend whenever they can and tell us what topics they would like.
Do our best always to be well staffed and equipped. This is an expensive exercise.	Pay fees promptly to keep costs down.

Signed .... **Parent**

.... **Nursery Manager**

WORKING WITH YOUR OWN MANAGERS

Unless you are proprietor of your own nursery, you will probably be answerable to some form of management system, whether an individual or a committee. When the management is undertaken by a committee there will normally be a chairperson with whom you are likely to have most contact, often on a quite informal basis. However it is arranged, it is important that the relationship between you be characterised by honesty, trust and support. If you are considering taking on the management of a nursery, you must be sure that you will be able to work well with your own manager(s) and that you share their philosophy. If the relationship between you goes wrong, the amount of unhappiness generated is a very serious for all concerned – including the children.

> You must be sure you will be able to work well with your managers and share their philosophy

You will need to:

● Provide clear, accurate information, both formally through written reports, often presented at meetings, and informally by phone or in discussion.

● Have a full set of nursery policies which management has had a hand in designing and approving and to which reference can be made in the case of any difficulties.

● Keep your administrative records in good order so that information is readily retrievable. This is particularly important in the case of financial records.

● Present your development plans persuasively with all costings and staffing implications worked out.

● Seek approval before implementing major change.

● Make sure you are sufficiently knowledgeable about existing, impending or possible legislation which might affect the nursery by keeping up to date through reading and attending any briefing meetings arranged by the local authority, so that you are in a position to advise.

For your part, you have a right to:

● Expect the trust and support of your employer(s) unless and until you commit any serious breach of trust yourself.

● Assessment of your work performance.

LIAISON WITH THE LOCAL AUTHORITY

You will be regularly monitored and inspected by local authority representatives, normally from the social services daycare department (though, depending on your status, you may be responsible to the Department for Education and Employment in whole or in part). Their role is not adversarial: they are normally happy to advise and support you, to aid with your training, information, grant seeking and networking. It is important to maintain good relations with them: they are a valuable resource help and information.

LIAISON WITH LOCAL COMMUNITY

There is a danger that children in full-time nursery do not get 'out and about' en
They need to learn something of the wider environment and the world of work.

- **Take them on purposeful visits:**
  To shops to purchase food for cooking.
  To the library to borrow books.
  as well as on recreational expeditions:
  To the park to feed the ducks.
  On bus or train journeys for the experience.
  To the theatre for the older ones.
  To the local gym for baby bounce sessions.
- The local library is a very valuable resource. By using it, you suggest that
  value books. Children's librarians often have a programme of storytelling ar
  arrange for bulk borrowing of books for under-fives groups.
- Being seen on walks with the children from your nursery is a way of adve
  your existence within the locality to business people who may help you with
  tions (see chapter three) and to potential clients.
- Ask people into the nursery to talk to the children about various aspects o
  a community police officer, dentist or dental nurse, podiatrist or shoe shop
  sentative, a parent with a hobby or craft that the children could relate to. F
  brainstorming session to think of more.

advant
of trair
your c
staff is
it enab
you
prom
unquali
s

LIAISON WITH LOCAL SCHOOLS

Current Government policy is pointing towards linking preschool experience w
early stages of the National Curriculum by stating targets that five-year-olds st
school should already have achieved. Providers in voucher schemes will be ag
to take on four-year-old targets. It is also clear that children adapt far better
stresses of starting school when they have some prior knowledge of and introc
to it. So, though it is not always possible to have direct contact with the schoc
feed, awareness of the next stage is important. Parents should be encourag
take children to their new school in advance of their first day there as part of ar
duction process.

Where it is possible to liaise directly, ask the head teacher for an appointmer
about her hopes and expectations for the children joining the school. You ma
sider asking parents to pass on to the school records that you have kept on ii
ual children in order to promote continuity in their children's early experience.

You may well have an agreement with the local secondary school whereb
send older pupils for work experience. This can work well, but you need to
clearly defined expectations of each other. Discussion with the teacher in cha
the project is very important.

LIAISON WITH TRAINING ESTABLISHMENTS

Having students on training should give you:
- An extra pair of hands.
- A young, enthusiastic and energetic helper.
- An increased range of adult contact children can enjoy.
- The chance, through contacts with the college, to keep in touch with professional developments and other professionals.
- An atmosphere in which your staff will be 'kept on their toes' as they may be called on to explain their practice to the student and will have to clarify their thinking.
- The chance to appear a responsible institution.

Your contribution will be:
- Being in charge of and helping assess the student.
- Taking your share of training the next generation of childcare staff.

TYPES OF IN-SERVICE TRAINING

As well as taking NNEB trainees, many nursery managers either become National Vocational Qualification (NVQ) assessors themselves or send a member of staff on a course to become one. The status of Registered Assessor can be achieved through training at a local assessment centre (see Useful Addresses for that of CACHE), practical demonstration of competence in a work setting and presentation of a portfolio of evidence. Once competence has been achieved, Registered Assessors will need to attend occasional meetings at their centres to stay up to date.

The advantage to a nursery of being able to train its own staff – and perhaps external candidates as well – is that it enables them to promote good unqualified staff to qualified status. It also engenders dynamism into the nursery if it is to be used as a setting for 'good practice' and enables the nursery, via the assessor, to be kept in touch with professional developments.

Other in-house training may be part of what a nursery manager thinks will be valuable to help staff keep their ideas fresh or simply to gain practice in areas in which they are rusty.

ADVANCED AWARD-BEARING TRAINING

Managers should encourage staff, through part or whole payment of their fees, to attend advanced courses such as the Advanced Diploma in Childcare and Education, which requires attendance at evening classes in a providing college (or, if this is hard to manage, Open University versions) and carrying out assignments at the workplace. The benefit will be considerable extra skills for the children.

NETWORKING

Contact with fellow practitioners is invaluable both professionally and recreationally. The local authority will probably run a programme of under-eights sessions; these are useful in themselves and good meeting places to swop 'shop'.

One relatively new initiative is for nurseries to group into a local network. One group of nurseries in the Berkshire/Hampshire border area reports excitedly about the advantages it has gained in working this way. Managers say that it's nice to know that someone else will be on the end of a telephone line who will understand problems, be sympathetic and perhaps offer some good advice. Other advantages are:

- Mutual support at other staff levels.
- Opportunities to identify joint in-service training needs and the chance to share in-house systems or buy in experts and share the cost.
- Visiting each other's nurseries enables everyone to gain fresh ideas. You can even organise staff exchanges.
- Expensive items of equipment can be bought jointly and shared. More favourable terms can sometimes be negotiated with suppliers if you group together to bulk purchase renewables.
- Simply socialising together.

Appendices

APPENDIX ONE

An employee must be provided with a written statement setting out the main particulars of her employment (see chapter two). This pro forma is reproduced by permission of Waterlow Business Supplies (see Useful Addresses).

STATEMENT OF TERMS OF EMPLOYMENT

This Statement is issued pursuant to Section 26
of the Trade Union Reform and Employment Rights Act 1993.

Date of Statement: ....

NAME OF EMPLOYMENT: ....

COMPANY NAME:
....
Your employment began on:.......................................
Your period of continuous
employment began on: ....

JOB TITLE: ....

PLACE OF WORK: ....

PAY:
Basic rate of pay £ .... per.........................
Details of other pay or benefits (if applicable):
....
....
....
Pay Intervals: ....

HOURS OF WORK: ....

HOLIDAY ENTITLEMENT: ....days per annum excluding public holidays.*
Holidays must be taken in the year from ....
to ....
Details of holiday pay (where different from the basic

94

rate of pay above) and entitlement of accrued holiday pay on the termination of employment:

....

....

SICKNESS: Terms and conditions relating to incapacity for work due to sickness or injury and provisions for sick pay are attached/may be obtained from*

....

....

PENSIONS: *Provisions relating to pensions and pension schemes are attached/may be obtained from*

....

There are no provisions relating to pensions or pension schemes. A contract-out certificate is/is not in force for this employment.

DISCIPLINE: Rules concerning discipline are attached/may be obtained from*

....

....

You are entitled to appeal against any disciplinary decision taken against you.
Any appeal should be made in writing within .... working days to

....

GRIEVANCE: The person to whom you should apply if you have a grievance relating to your employment is

....

You may be asked to provide details of the grievance in writing.
Details of the procedure are attached.

NOTICE: *You are required to give the following notice:

....

....

*You are entitled to receive the following notice:

....

....

The notice you must give and are entitled to receive are as given in the relevant collective agreement specified below/under s49 of the Employment Protection (Consolidation) Act 1978.

The above periods of notice also apply where the employment is temporary or where the employment is to be terminated before the end of a fixed term.

TERM OF EMPLOYMENT:
(Where employment is temporary or for a fixed term)

....

....

COLLECTIVE AGREEMENTS:
The following collective agreements apply in respect of your employment:

....

....

WORK OUTSIDE THE UNITED KINGDOM:
*You will not be required to work outside the United Kingdom.

*Where you are required to work outside the United Kingdom for more than one month the following terms apply:

....

....

....

....

....

* Delete as applicable.

I acknowledge receipt of this Statement of Terms

Employee's signature:..Date received:..........................

APPENDIX TWO

A regular staff meeting is an important way of ensuring good staff management and inter-staff communications (see chapter two). This is an example how one nursery planned and minuted one of their staff meetings.

Larksmead Nursery School – Manager Sophie McNeigh
Staff meeting to be held Monday 12th November 6 - 7.15 pm followed by take away buffet supper.

AGENDA

1. Minutes of the last meeting
2. New system of record keeping reports   room 1
      room 2
      room 3

3. Ideas for Parents' Evening
4. Next development programme
5. Any other business (AOB)
6. Date of next meeting

MINUTES

Present: JS, ML, LB,
MP, SN, RA, FL, AR, RC, SMcN.
Apologies: FN and PS.

1. The minutes of the last meeting were read and accepted.
2. Agenda Item 2

● Everybody agreed that the new record keeping system meant that key staff were more aware of their children's developmental stage. Marianne L. said it had helped her to have the records when discussing Anthony's progress with his parents. It had helped her to explain the future programme she was planning for him.

● Three people agreed about its usefulness but complained about the very high increase in workload as a result of implementing the new systems.

● Sophie asked by how much the workload had increased and was told that it meant at least two extra hours in the working week. She promised to put the matter to the Management Committee and request that one hour per member of staff non-contact time be arranged. She would be able to advise staff of the results by the next staff meeting. She would cite recent research highlighting the need for non-contact time if records are to be well maintained.

3. Agenda Item 3
Several suggestions were put forward. These included:

   a. Managing children's behaviour – In-house speaker.
   b. The importance of involving children in the things that adults do with an out-side speaker.
   c. Getting ready for school.

It was decided to adopt (a) because many members of staff had been approached by parents on this very issue.

Sophie would do a lead talk while Janice and Monique said they would like to use a case-study exercise with parents participating. It was agreed to publicise the evening for Monday 18th January. Anna asked about refreshments and it was agreed that the nursery should charge £1 to cover the cost of coffee/tea and biscuits.

4. Agenda Item 4
Sophie congratulated staff on their successful implementation of the new record keeping system. She then asked staff to give their ideas for this year's development programme. After some discussion everyone agreed they would like to develop 'science through play'.

The new programme would require some in-service training, professional reading and the acquisition of new resources.

By the next meeting staff should have ideas on how and by whom they would like their training organized.

Once the training was completed they should then be able to see what new resources should be purchased.

5. AOB
Francine asked whether it would be possible to speak with the local college lecturer re NNEB placements. Sophie said she would arrange this.

Melanie asked for the Christmas cards to be made available early this year.

6. Date of next meeting – 12th December
Meeting closed 7.30 spot on!

APPENDIX THREE

Appraisal is not an external assessment of performance but a valuable way of helping members of staff develop and improve their professional skills (see chapter two). Below are some grading guidelines and criteria for appraisal.

Grading

1. Consistently reaches a very high standard in all areas.
2. Usually reaches a high standard in all or almost all of the areas.
3. Generally satisfactory but with some shortcomings.
4. Generally unsatisfactory with serious shortcomings (though it must be recognised that the person could have isolated strengths).

Criteria for a grade 1 in the major areas of professionalism in the childcare and education field:

Managers may feel the need to modify some of these slightly in the light of their own circumstances. Appraisers should be able to deduce when individuals should be assessed at grades 2, 3 or 4.

Professional attitude

- Is proud of her profession and appreciates the extreme importance of the work she does.
- Is knowledgeable and reflects on her own performance.
- Consistently punctual and gives herself sufficient time to prepare thoroughly for the day's routines and activities.
- Attendance is regular.
- Is keen to keep herself professionally updated through reading about new developments and attending staff meetings and appropriate training courses.
- Demonstrates enthusiasm.
- Supports others, including students.
- Suggests and contributes own ideas.
- Is loyal, discreet and keeps confidences.

Relationships with children

- Consistently shows concern for the all-round development of all the children in her care.
- Interacts well with children, attends to what they say or try to communicate, and communicates effectively with them, using good quality language.
- Is sensitive to the needs of children and respects them.
- Supports children in their quest for independence and encourages their various endeavours.

- Maintains established boundaries for behaviour and is fair and consistent in their application.
- Promotes children's confidence and the development of a positive self-image.

Planning and carrying out activities with children
- Observes safety requirements at all times.
- Uses individual children's records to inform planning.
- Plans activities carefully as part of a broad and balanced curriculum.
- Gathers resources together to support the activities.
- Gives careful consideration to appropriate group size.
- Is able to demonstrate particular skills when these are needed.
- Matches activities to different levels of maturation.
- Accepts and encourages children's own ideas within the activity.
- Ensures that activities are both set up and put away carefully, involving the children where possible.

Ability to work effectively with parents
- Is consistently friendly and approachable.
- Is able to communicate with parents on:
  The child's progress
  The aims and philosophy of the nursery
  How children learn and develop.
- Listens to parents' concerns and provides advice and support when asked.
- Involves parents in the compilation of their children's records.
- Keeps confidences (within legal constraints).

Ability to work with other members of the team
- Is consistently friendly and co-operative with other team members in planning, working and evaluating together.
- Is prepared to take her fair share of the rough with the smooth.
- Will support colleagues who need help.
- Accepts criticism constructively.
- Listens to other people's point of view and contributes her own.
- Is open and honest in her dealings with others.

Maintenance of the environment
- Works consistently helping to maintain a safe, interesting and orderly environment.
- Uses and develops the outdoor environment as fully as possible.
- Is keen to contribute own efforts in resource collection and maintenance.
- Contributes own ideas and efforts in producing displays.

APPENDIX FOUR

The School Curriculum and Assessment Authority (SCAA) published *Desirable outcomes for children's learning on entering compulsory education* in January 1996. These are reproduced here by permission.

Personal and social development

Children are confident, show appropriate self respect and are able to establish effective relationships with other children and adults. They work as part of a group and independently, are able to concentrate and persevere in their learning and to seek help where needed. They are eager to explore new learning and show the ability to initiate ideas and to solve simple practical problems. They demonstrate independence in selecting an activity or resources and in dressing and personal hygiene.

Children are sensitive to the needs and feelings of others and show respect for people of other cultures and beliefs. They take turns and share fairly. They express their feelings and behave in appropriate ways, developing an understanding of what is right, what is wrong and why. They treat living things, property and their environment with care and concern. They respond to relevant cultural and religious events and show a range of feelings, such as wonder, joy or sorrow, in response to their experiences of the world.

Language and literacy

In small and large groups, children listen attentively and talk about their experiences. They use a growing vocabulary with increasing fluency to express thoughts and convey meaning to the listener. They listen and respond to stories, songs, nursery rhymes and poems. They make up their own stories and take part in role play with confidence.

Children enjoy books and handle them carefully, understanding how they are organised. They know that words and pictures carry meaning and that, in English, print is read from left to right and from top to bottom. They begin to associate sounds with patterns in rhymes, with syllables, and with words and letters. They recognise their own names and some familiar words. They recognise letters of the alphabet by shape and sound. In their writing they use pictures, symbols, familiar words and letters, to communicate meaning, showing awareness of some of the different purposes of writing. They write their names with appropriate use of upper and lower case letters.

Mathematics

Children use mathematical language, such as circle, in front of, bigger than and more, to describe shape, position, size and quantity. They recognise and recreate patterns. They are familiar with number, rhymes, songs, stories, counting games and activities. They compare, sort, match, order, sequence and count using everyday objects. They recognise and use numbers to ten and are familiar with larger numbers from their everyday lives. They begin to use their developing mathematical understanding to solve practical problems. Through practical activities children understand and record numbers, begin to show awareness of number operations, such as addition and subtraction, and begin to use the language involved.

Knowledge and understanding of the world
Children talk about where they live, their environment, their families and past and present events in their own lives. They explore and recognise features of living things, objects and events in the natural and made world and look closely at similarities, differences, patterns and change. They show an awareness of the purposes of some features of the area in which they live. They talk about their observations, sometimes recording them, and ask questions to gain information about why things happen and how things work. They explore and select materials and equipment and use skills such as cutting, joining, folding and building for a variety of purposes. They use technology, where appropriate, to support their learning.

Physical development
Children move confidently and imaginatively with increasing control and co-ordination and an awareness of space and others. They use a range of small and large equipment and balancing and climbing apparatus, with increasing skill. They handle appropriate tools, objects, construction and malleable materials safely and with increasing control.

Creative development
Children explore sound and colour, texture, shape, form and space in two and three dimensions. They respond in a variety of ways to what they see, hear, smell, touch and feel. Through art, music, dance, stories and imaginative play, they show an increasing ability to use their imagination, to listen and to observe. They use a widening range of materials, suitable tools, instruments and other resources to express ideas and to communicate their feelings.

The full copy of *Desirable outcomes* and of *Nursery education scheme – the next steps* (published by the Department for Education and Employment) and more information on nursery education may be obtained from the Department or by ringing 01345 543345.

Useful addresses

Advisory, Conciliation and Arbitration Service (ACAS)
83 Euston Road
London NW1 2RB
(0171 396 0022 – for regional offices, see telephone book)

Association of British Insurers
51 Gresham Street
London EC2V 7HQ
(0171 600 3333)

BAPs Health Publication Unit
Storage and Distribution Centre
Heywood Stores
Manchester Road
Heywood
Lancs OL10 2PZ
(01706 366287)

British Association for Early Childhood Education (BAECE)
111 City View House
463 Bethnal Green Road
London E2 9QY
(0171 739 7594)

British Insurance and Investment Brokers Association
14 Bevis Marks
London EC3A 7NT
(0171 623 9043)

CACHE
8 Chequer Street
St Albans

Herts AL1 3XZ
(01727 867333)

Child Accident Prevention Trust
4th Floor
Clerks Court
18-20 Farringdon Lane
London EC1R 3AU
(0171 608 3828)
(*Accident Prevention in daycare and play settings:* book, £6.50; training book, £14.95 plus training and consultancy services)

Department for Education and Employment
Sanctuary Buildings
Great Smith Street
Westminster
London SW1P 3BT
0171 925 5000
(0171 925 5555 for public enquiries relating to the requirements or administration of the voucher scheme)

Department of Health
Skipton House
80 London Road
Elephant and Castle
London SE1 6LW
(0171 972 2000)

Department of Trade and Industry
1 Victoria Street
London SW1H 0ET
(0171 215 5000)

USEFUL ADDRESSES

The Directory of Grant Making Trusts
Kings Hill
West Malling
Kent ME19 4TA
(01732 520000)

Eaton Publications
Eaton House
PO Box 34
Walton-on-Thames
Surrey KT12 1LN
(01932 229001)

Equal Opportunities Commission
Overseas House
Quay Street
Manchester M3 3HN
(0161 833 9244)
NW1 3AL (071 383 5455).

Health Education Authority
Hamilton House,
Mabledon Place,
London WC1H 9TX
(0171 383 3833).

HMSO Publications Centre
PO Box 276
London SW8 5DT
0171 873 0011)

The Industrial Society
Robert Hyde House
48 Bryanston Square
London W1H 7LN
(0171 262 2401)
(Members of the society can use its
consultancy, training and information
services)

The Institute of Management
Management House
Cottingham Road
Corby
NN17 1TT
01536 204222

National Children's Bureau
Under Fives Unit
8 Wakley Street
London EC1V 7QE
(0171 843 6000)

**National Council for Vocational
Qualifications (NCVQ)**
222 Euston Road
London NW1 2BZ
(0171 387 9898)

**National Private Day Nurseries
Association**
Dennis House
Hawley Road
Hinchley
Leicestershire LE10 OPR
(0455 635556)

Personal Investment Authority
(formerly Fimbra)
Hertsmere House
Hertsmere Road
London E14 4AB
(0171 538 8860)

Preschool Learning Alliance
61-63 Kings Cross Road
London WC1X 9LL
(0171 833 0991)

Professional Association of Nursery Nurses (PANN)
2 St James's Court
77 Friar Gate
Derby DE1 1BT
(013323 43029)

School Curriculum and Assessment Authority
Newcombe House
45 Notting Hill Gate
London W11 3JB
(0171 229 1234)

St John Ambulance Association
1 Grovesnor Crescent
London SW1X 7EF
(0171 235 5231)

Waterlow Business Supplies
Freepost MK 904
Bletchley
Milton Keynes
MK1 1UJ
(01908 647788)
(For personnel forms)

NOTES

NOTES

NOTES

NOTES

NOTES

NOTES